EFFORTLESS ONLINE INCOME

Unveiling the Secrets of Thriving in the
Virtual Work Realm

Jeffery Friedman

Table of Contents

CHAPTER 1

INTRODUCTION

Why Choose the Thrilling Path of Online Employment?

In this chapter, we will delve into the exciting world of online employment, exploring the myriad reasons why it's a path worth considering. Online employment has transformed the way we work, offering a range of opportunities and benefits that are often too compelling to ignore. In the following sections, we will break down the key reasons why individuals are increasingly drawn to this dynamic and flexible way of earning a living.

1. Unprecedented Flexibility:

The Freedom to Define Your Schedule: Online employment offers the unique advantage of setting your work hours. Whether you're an early bird or a night owl, you can tailor your work schedule to align with your personal preferences and peak productivity times. This flexibility is particularly appealing to individuals who value autonomy in their daily routines.

Balancing Work and Life on Your Terms: Achieving work-life balance is often a struggle in traditional jobs, but online employment allows you to strike a harmonious balance between your professional and personal life. You have the freedom to attend to family needs, pursue hobbies, and maintain a healthy lifestyle while still meeting work commitments.

Embracing Remote Work as a Lifestyle: Remote work is more than just a job; it's a lifestyle choice. It enables you to escape the confines of a traditional office and embrace a location-independent way of life. Whether you're working from home, a coffee shop, or a beachside villa, you can adapt your work environment to suit your preferences.

2. Diverse Range of Opportunities:

Exploring the Multifaceted World of Online Jobs: Online employment encompasses a wide range of job opportunities, from freelance writing and graphic design to virtual assistance and digital marketing. This diversity allows individuals to choose careers that align with their interests, skills, and passions.

Niche Specializations: Finding Your Unique Path: Within the online job market, there are numerous niche specializations waiting to be explored. Whether you have expertise in a specific field or a passion for a particular industry, online employment offers the chance to carve out a unique career path.

3. Location Independence:

Breaking Free from Geographic Limitations: Online employment eliminates the need to be tied to a specific geographic location. You can work for clients or companies from around the world, opening up a global job market that transcends borders.

The Appeal of Working from Anywhere: The ability to work from anywhere is a major draw for many individuals. Whether you're traveling, relocating, or simply seeking a change of scenery, online employment allows you to maintain your income while enjoying new experiences.

4. Financial Rewards:

Unveiling the Potential for Earning Online: Online employment can be financially rewarding, with the potential for competitive salaries and income growth. This section delves into the various ways individuals can earn money online, from traditional employment to entrepreneurial ventures.

Diversifying Income Streams in the Virtual World: Online employment often allows for multiple income streams, such as freelancing, consulting, and passive income. Readers will learn how to leverage these opportunities to build a more stable financial future.

Comparing Salaries: Offline vs. Online: A comparison between salaries in traditional jobs and online employment provides insights into the earning potential of each. This analysis helps readers understand the financial advantages of choosing online employment.

5. Career Growth and Skill Development:

Acquiring In-Demand Skills for the Digital Age: Online employment encourages individuals to develop skills that are highly sought after in the digital age. From digital marketing to remote collaboration, readers will discover how online work can enhance their skill set.

Career Advancement and Long-Term Prospects: In the realm of online jobs, career advancement and long-term prospects are shaped by a meritocratic environment where talent and effort are rewarded. This dynamic landscape fosters rapid skill development, provides networking opportunities with a global reach, and often serves as a springboard for entrepreneurial ventures. However, the path to advancement requires strong self-management and may involve intense competition. Long-term prospects in online work are buoyed by the growth of digital industries, the ability to build a robust portfolio, global opportunities, and adaptability. Challenges include income variability and potential isolation, making it essential for individuals to practice financial planning and maintain a support network for lasting career satisfaction. Overall, success in online careers hinges on dedication, adaptability, and a commitment to continuous learning.

Learning as You Earn: Learning as you earn" in online jobs means you can keep gaining new skills and knowledge while you work and make money. It's like getting paid to learn and grow in your job. Online jobs often require you to stay updated with the latest technology and trends, so you're always improving yourself while making a living. It's a way to make your job even more rewarding by becoming better at what you do over time.

6. Work-Life Integration:

Achieving a Harmonious Work-Life Balance: Achieving a harmonious work-life balance in online jobs means finding a way to manage your work and personal life so they fit together well and make you feel happy. It's about making sure your job doesn't take up all your time and energy, so you can also enjoy your life outside of work. Online jobs offer flexibility that can help you create this balance, allowing you to work when it suits you and still have time for family, hobbies, and relaxation, which makes life more enjoyable.

Overcoming Burnout: Overcoming burnout in online jobs means finding ways to prevent feeling very tired or stressed from too much work. When you work online, it's important to manage your time well, take breaks, and make sure you don't work too much without rest. Burnout can happen if you don't take care of yourself, but with the right balance, you can stay energized and motivated in your online work.

The Role of Wellbeing in the Virtual Workspace: The role of wellbeing in the virtual workspace means how important it is to take care of your health and happiness while working online. In online jobs, you have to look after your physical and mental well-being because you might not have colleagues or an office environment to support you. It's about staying healthy, managing stress, and creating a positive work atmosphere for yourself, which can lead to better job satisfaction and performance.

7. Entrepreneurial Ventures:

Online Business Ventures: Online business ventures mean starting and running a business on the internet. It's like having a store or service that people can access through their computers or phones. Online businesses can include selling products, offering services, or even creating and selling digital products like e-books or software. They provide opportunities to reach a global audience and can be started with relatively low costs, making them an attractive option for entrepreneurs.

The Appeal of Building Digital Empires: The appeal of building digital empires means the excitement and potential rewards of creating big and successful businesses online. It's like building a powerful online brand or platform that can reach many people and generate income. Online entrepreneurs dream of making a big impact and earning substantial profits through their digital ventures, which can include e-commerce stores, popular websites, or influential social media channels. This appeal comes from the idea that the internet offers vast opportunities for growth and success.

Case Studies: Successful Online Entrepreneurs:

Case studies of successful online entrepreneurs are like real-life stories about people who have done very well with their internet businesses. These stories show how regular individuals turned their online ideas into successful money-making ventures. By looking at these cases, people can learn valuable lessons and get inspired to start their own online businesses, hoping to achieve similar success.

8. Adapting to the Future of Work:

The Transformative Impact of Technology: The transformative impact of technology means how much technology has changed and improved our lives. In online jobs, technology plays a big role because it helps people work and communicate over the internet. It makes it possible to do many things faster and more efficiently, like connecting with people worldwide, automating tasks, and creating new job opportunities. Technology keeps evolving and changing how we work and live, and it's a big part of online jobs.

Preparing for the Evolving Job Landscape: Preparing for the evolving job landscape means getting ready for changes in the types of jobs that are available. In online jobs, the job landscape is always changing because of technology and other factors. This means people need to keep learning and adapting to new skills and ways of working. By staying flexible and open to change, you can be better prepared for future job opportunities and challenges in the online world.

Why Online Employment is Here to Stay: Why online employment is here to stay means that working online is not just a temporary trend; it's going to be a permanent way of working. The internet and technology keep growing, and more and more jobs are moving online. People are finding the benefits of online work, like flexibility and global opportunities, too good to give up. So, online employment is likely to keep growing and becoming a significant part of the job world for a long time.

Navigating the World of Online Jobs with Expertise

The online job market is like a big digital marketplace where people look for work and businesses search for employees or freelancers to do tasks or projects. It's similar to a giant online job fair, but it's open all the time, not just on certain dates. In this market, you can find all sorts of jobs, like writing, designing, programming, customer service, and many others. It's not just for one type of work; it's for a whole bunch of different jobs you can do using the internet.

How It Works:
In the online job market, there are websites and platforms where you can look for jobs or offer your skills. You can create a profile that shows what you can do and what experience you have.

Employers or clients post job listings, and you can apply for the ones that match your skills and interests. It's a bit like online shopping, but instead of buying things, you're looking for work or hiring someone to do a job.

Benefits:
One of the cool things about the online job market is that it's super flexible. You can often work from anywhere, like your home, a coffee shop, or even while traveling. Plus, there are jobs for people with all sorts of backgrounds and skills, from beginners to experts. It's a bit like having a big menu of job options to choose from.

Challenges:
But, like anything, there are challenges too. Competition can be tough because lots of people are looking for online work. Sometimes, it might take a while to find the right job or gig. And, because you're not meeting your employer face-to-face, you need to be careful about scams

or dishonest people. It's important to do your research and be cautious.

The Future:
The online job market keeps growing as more businesses and workers discover the benefits of working online. So, understanding how it works and how to stand out in this digital job world can open up exciting opportunities for your career. It's a bit like learning the rules of a new game—once you get the hang of it, you can start playing and winning in the online job market.

CHAPTER 2

BUILDING THE FOUNDATIONS FOR SUCCESS

"Building the Foundations for Success" in the context of online jobs means laying the groundwork for a successful online career. It involves developing essential skills, creating a strong online presence, and establishing a reliable work routine. Just like a sturdy building needs a solid foundation to stand tall, online job seekers and professionals must build a strong foundation of skills, professionalism, and discipline to thrive in the digital work environment.

Digital Skill Development

In the world of online jobs, digital skill development is like learning how to use special tools for your job, but these tools are all on the computer. Imagine you want to be a great artist, but instead of using paint and brushes, you use digital art software on your computer. These skills are super important because they help you do your job well, and they can make you more attractive to employers or clients.

First, you need to identify which skills are important for the type of online job you want. For example, if you want to work in web design, you should learn about things like coding and graphic design software. If you want to write for websites, you'll need to know about digital content creation and SEO (search engine optimization). Many online courses and resources are available to help you learn these skills, and some are even free.

Second, digital skill development is not a one-time thing; it's more like a journey. You keep learning and improving your skills over time. The online world is always changing, so you have to stay updated with the latest trends and technologies in your field. This way, you can be the best at what you do and keep growing in your online job. So, think of digital skill development as your secret superpower in the online job market—it's what makes you a digital pro!

Picture digital skill development as building a toolbox for your online job. Each skill you learn is like adding a new tool to your toolbox. The more skills you have, the better equipped you are to tackle different tasks and challenges in your online career.

Let's say you're interested in online marketing. You might start by learning about social media advertising, email marketing, and data analysis. These skills help you promote products or services online and understand how well your marketing efforts are doing. As you get more experienced, you might dive deeper into specific areas like pay-per-click advertising or content marketing.

One great thing about digital skill development is that you can often learn at your own pace. There are online courses, tutorials, and communities where you can ask questions and share knowledge with others. Plus, when you apply these skills in your online job, you're not just learning—you're also earning money and gaining valuable experience. So, think of digital skill development as an exciting journey that empowers you to thrive in the digital job market, opening doors to new opportunities and career growth.

Creating a Winning Online Profile for Online Jobs

Imagine your online profile as your digital resume or business card in the world of online jobs. It's like a way to introduce yourself and show what you're good at to potential employers or clients. Just like you want to make a good first impression when you meet someone new, you want your online profile to impress those who might hire you.

To create a winning online profile, you need to showcase your skills and experience. It's a bit like telling a story about yourself. You should include details about what you've done in the past and what you're good at doing. If you've worked on projects or jobs that are related to the one you want, be sure to mention them. This helps people see that you have experience and can do the job well.

Your profile picture and bio are also important. Think of your picture as your online smile—it should be friendly and professional. Your bio is like a short introduction about yourself, so keep it clear and interesting. It's like saying, "Hi, I'm good at this, and here's why you should hire me." When your online profile is well-crafted, it can open doors to exciting online job opportunities, just like a great first impression can lead to new friendships.

Effective Online Communication

Effective online communication is like talking to your colleagues, clients, or customers through your computer or phone. Since you can't see or hear each other in person, you have to be really good at using written messages, emails, or video calls to make sure everyone understands and works together smoothly.

In online jobs, you need to write and talk clearly, just like when you talk face-to-face. Imagine you're sending an email to a client or coworker. It's important to use proper grammar and spelling, so they can easily understand what you're saying. Also, be polite and respectful in your messages, just like you would in a real conversation.

Another part of effective online communication is listening carefully to what others are saying. When you're on a video call or reading messages, pay attention and ask questions if you're not sure about something. It's a bit like being a good listener in a regular conversation. Good online communication helps you avoid misunderstandings, build trust, and work well with others, even if they're far away.

Time Management and Productivity

Time management and productivity in online jobs are like being good at managing your time and getting your work done efficiently when you work using your computer. Just like you have a schedule for your day, you need to plan when you'll work, when you'll take breaks, and when you'll finish.

Imagine you have a list of things to do for your online job, like answering emails, writing reports, or designing websites. You should organize your tasks and decide which ones to do first. It's a bit like making a to-do list and checking things off as you complete them. This way, you can make sure you finish your work on time and do it well.

It's also important to avoid distractions when you work online. Imagine if you're trying to read a book, but your phone keeps buzzing with messages. That can make it hard to concentrate. In online jobs, you need to find ways to stay focused, like turning off notifications or setting specific times for checking messages. Good time management and productivity help you do your job effectively and have more time for other things you enjoy.

I'd like to direct your attention to my previous book, 'Stress Management for Better Productivity.' In that comprehensive work, I delve even deeper into the very subject we've been discussing here. For a more detailed understanding and valuable insights on this matter, I encourage you to turn to 'Stress Management for Better Productivity,' where you'll find a wealth of information to enhance your knowledge. It serves as an excellent companion to our current discussion and offers a deeper dive into the strategies and concepts presented here.

Setting up a Home Office

Setting up a home office for online jobs means creating a special workspace in your home where you can work comfortably and efficiently using your computer. Think of it as your own little workplace right at home. This is really important because it helps you focus on your work and get things done just like you would in an office.

Choosing the Right Space: First, you need to find a good spot in your home for your home office. It could be a corner in a room, a spare room, or even a space in your living room. The important thing is that it's a place where you can work without too many distractions.

Getting the Right Equipment: Your computer is like your main tool for online jobs, so make sure it's in good shape. You might also need a comfortable chair to sit on for long hours. It's a bit like getting the right tools if you're a carpenter or a chef—you want things that help you do your job well.

Organizing Your Work: Once you have your home office set up, you should keep it neat and organized. This way, you can find what you need easily. Imagine if you're an artist—you wouldn't want to lose your paintbrushes or colors, right? So, keep your computer cables tidy, have a place for your papers, and make sure everything is in order.

Creating a Comfortable Environment: Your home office should also be a comfy place to work. You can decorate it with things that make you happy and motivated, like plants or pictures. Think of it as your own little creative space. It's a bit like making your room cozy and welcoming.

Having a well-organized and comfortable home office is like having a secret superpower for online jobs. It helps you work better and feel good while doing it, just like a superhero with the perfect headquarters!

Professionalism and Online Etiquette

Professionalism and online etiquette in online jobs are like the rules of being polite and respectful when you work on the internet. Just like you behave nicely when you meet people in person, you should do the same online. These things help you do your job well and build good relationships with others.

Clear Communication: When you talk to your colleagues, clients, or customers online, it's important to use clear and respectful language, just like you would in a face-to-face conversation. Imagine you're talking to your teacher or boss—you'd be polite and clear, right? That's the same online.

Punctuality: Being on time for online meetings or finishing your work when you promised is also a part of professionalism. Imagine if you were meeting a friend, and they were always late—it wouldn't feel nice. So, be punctual and reliable.

Respecting Differences: Online jobs often connect you with people from all over the world. It's important to respect their cultures and beliefs, just like you'd want your beliefs to be respected. This helps create a positive work environment.

Online Safety: When working online, you should also be careful with your personal information and avoid sharing it with strangers. It's a bit like keeping your home address private—you wouldn't want just anyone to know it.

Conflict Resolution: Sometimes, you might have disagreements with people online. It's important to resolve these conflicts calmly and respectfully, just like you'd want people to resolve disagreements with you. This keeps the work atmosphere friendly and productive.

Professionalism and online etiquette are like having good manners in the digital world. They help you work well with others and make online jobs a positive and respectful place to be. So, think of it as being a kind and respectful online friend to your colleagues and clients!

Building a Personal Brand

Building a personal brand in online jobs is like creating your own unique identity or reputation on the internet. Imagine it's like being a superhero with your own logo and superpowers. This personal brand shows who you are, what you're good at, and what people can expect from you when they work with you online.

Understanding Your Brand: The first step is to think about what makes you special and what you want to be known for in your online career. It's a bit like deciding what kind of superhero you want to be. Do you want to be known for your creativity, your problem-solving skills, or your friendliness? This helps you stand out.

Consistency: Once you know what your personal brand is, it's important to be consistent. This means you should show the same qualities and personality online all the time. Just like how superheroes always act like themselves, you should too. If you're known for being reliable, make sure you're always reliable.

Online Presence: Your online presence is like your superhero costume. It includes your social media profiles, your website (if you have one), and how you talk and write online. Make sure everything shows your personal brand. If you're known for being creative, share your creative work online.

Sharing Your Expertise: Showcasing your skills and knowledge in your field is like using your superpowers. Share helpful tips and advice with others online. Write articles, create videos, or join discussions related to your area of expertise. This helps people recognize your skills and trust you.

Networking: Just like superheroes team up with other heroes, you can network with other professionals online. Connect with people in your industry, join online groups, and be friendly and helpful. Building a network of contacts can open up new opportunities in your online career.

Building a personal brand is like creating a strong online identity that sets you apart and helps you succeed in your online job. It's a bit like being a superhero with your own unique style and powers, ready to make a positive impact in the online world.

Remote Work Ethics

Remote work ethics in online jobs are like the rules and principles that guide how you behave and work when you're not physically at an office but instead work from home or another location using the internet. It's a bit like having a set of good manners and rules to follow while working online, just like you would in a traditional workplace.

Responsibility: Being responsible is a big part of remote work ethics. It means you're accountable for your tasks and deadlines, just like you would be if you were in an office. Imagine if you promised your friend you'd meet them at a certain time—you wouldn't want to let them down. The same goes for your work tasks.

Honesty: Honesty is like telling the truth and being straightforward. It's important to be honest about your work progress, challenges you face, and any issues that come up. If you're having trouble with a task, it's better to let your team know instead of trying to hide it.

Communication: Good communication is key in remote work. You should keep your team and boss updated about your work, ask questions when you're unsure, and respond to messages and emails promptly. It's a bit like having a conversation with someone—you wouldn't want to ignore them.

Respect for Privacy: When you work from home, you should also respect your own and your colleagues' privacy. This means not snooping around in other people's work or personal matters and keeping your work-related information safe and secure.

Data Security: Keeping work-related data and information safe is another aspect of remote work ethics. Imagine if you had a secret recipe for your favorite dish—you wouldn't want it to get into the wrong hands. The same goes for work data; it should be protected from unauthorized access.

Adhering to Company Policies: Just like an office has rules, remote work often comes with company policies. It's important to read and follow these policies, whether it's about work hours, data protection, or any other rules set by your employer.

Remote work ethics help create a positive and respectful online work environment. They ensure that everyone can work together effectively, even if they are miles apart. Think of it as being a responsible and trustworthy online coworker who follows good online work manners.

Goal Setting and Career Planning

Goal setting and career planning in online jobs are like making a map for your professional journey on the internet. It's a bit like planning a trip—you decide where you want to go and how you're going to get there. In online jobs, this helps you stay focused, grow, and achieve your dreams.

Defining Your Goals: The first step is to figure out what you want to achieve in your online career. These are your goals. It's like deciding if you want to travel to the beach or the mountains. For example, you might aim to become a top web designer or earn a certain amount of money online.

Short-term and Long-term Goals: Goals can be short-term (like what you want to achieve this month) or long-term (what you want to achieve in a year or more). Think of short-term goals like stops on your journey and long-term goals as your final destination.

Creating a Plan: Once you have your goals, you need a plan to reach them. It's like planning your route for your trip. You might need to learn new skills, gain experience, or save money. Your plan helps you take small steps toward your big goals.

Assessing Progress: Just like checking a map to see if you're on the right path, you should regularly review your progress. Are you getting closer to your goals? If not, you might need to adjust your plan or work a bit harder.

Being Adaptable: Sometimes, the journey doesn't go exactly as planned. That's okay! Being adaptable means you can change your plans when needed, just like changing your route if you hit a roadblock during your trip.

Seeking Guidance: It's like asking for directions when you're lost during a trip. Don't be afraid to seek advice from experienced online professionals or mentors. They can offer valuable insights to help you reach your goals faster.

Staying Motivated: Keeping your motivation high is crucial. It's like staying excited about your trip. Remind yourself why you started this journey and celebrate your achievements along the way.

Goal setting and career planning help you turn your online job into a rewarding and successful adventure. They guide you in the right direction, help you stay on course, and ensure you reach the destinations you've set for your online career journey.

Health and Wellbeing in the Virtual Workspace

Health and wellbeing in the virtual workspace for online jobs are like taking care of yourself while working on your computer from home. Just like you need to eat well and exercise to stay healthy, it's important to look after yourself when working online.

Physical Health: Sitting at your computer for long hours can be like sitting for a long car ride. It's not good for your body. So, it's important to take breaks, stretch, and move around. You can do exercises or simply stand up and walk around for a few minutes to keep your body feeling good.

Ergonomics: Your workspace setup is important. It's like having a comfy chair and good lighting for reading a book. You should have an ergonomic chair and a desk that's at the right height to avoid straining your back or neck. Your computer screen should be at eye level to reduce strain on your eyes.

Mental Health: Just like you need to relax and de-stress after a busy day, it's important to manage your mental health while working online. Take breaks to clear your mind, practice deep breathing, or meditate. If you ever feel overwhelmed, it's okay to talk to someone about it, like a friend or a mental health professional.

Avoiding Burnout: Burnout is when you feel exhausted and stressed from working too much. It's like running a marathon without taking a break. To avoid burnout, set clear work hours, and don't overwork yourself. It's important to have a balance between work and personal life, just like balancing a see-saw.

Nutrition and Hydration: Eating well and staying hydrated are like putting good fuel in your car. It helps your body and brain function properly. Try to have healthy meals and drink enough water throughout the day.

Social Connection: Working online can sometimes make you feel isolated, like being alone on an island. It's important to stay connected with friends, family, and colleagues. Social interaction helps reduce loneliness and boosts your mood.

Time Management: Managing your time well is like having a schedule for your daily activities. It helps you avoid rushing and reduces stress.

Prioritize your tasks and make sure to include breaks in your schedule.

Taking care of your health and wellbeing while working online is like making sure your body and mind are in good shape for the journey of your online job. It helps you stay productive, feel better, and enjoy your work more.

CHAPTER 3
FREELANCING

Freelancing in online jobs means working independently as a self-employed professional. It's like being your own boss. Instead of having a traditional full-time job with one employer, you offer your skills and services to various clients or companies on a project-by-project basis. It's a bit like being a freelance writer who writes articles for different magazines or websites, or a freelance graphic designer who creates logos for different businesses. Freelancers often have more flexibility in their work schedules and can choose the projects they want to work on.

Getting Started as a Freelancer

Getting started as a freelancer in online jobs is like taking your first step into a world where you work independently and offer your skills to different clients or companies. It's a bit like starting your own small business where you are the boss. Here's a closer look at how to begin your journey as a freelancer:

1. Exploring the Freelancing Landscape:
Imagine you're an explorer discovering a new land. In freelancing, you start by exploring what kind of work you want to do and what skills you have. This helps you figure out where you fit in the world of freelancing.

2. Identifying Your Skills and Expertise:
Think of this as understanding what you're really good at. It could be writing, designing, coding, or any other skill. Knowing your strengths helps you find the right freelancing opportunities.

3. Creating a Standout Freelancer Profile:
Just like having a unique costume sets a superhero apart, your freelancer profile is your way of standing out. You'll create an online

profile that tells potential clients who you are, what you can do, and why they should hire you.

4. Building a Portfolio:

A portfolio is like a collection of your best work. It's your way of showing clients what you can do. You'll gather examples of your past projects and display them to demonstrate your skills and abilities.

5. Finding Your First Freelance Jobs:

Getting your first freelance job is a bit like catching your first fish. You'll look for freelance job platforms or websites where clients post projects. Then, you'll send proposals to clients who need your services.

6. Pricing Your Freelance Work:

Imagine you're setting a fair price for something you're selling. As a freelancer, you'll decide how much to charge for your services. You'll consider factors like your skills, experience, and the complexity of the project.

7. Delivering High-Quality Work:
Just like a superhero never lets down their city, you'll make sure to deliver top-notch work to your clients. This builds trust and can lead to more opportunities in the future.

8. Building Client Relationships:
Freelancers often work with different clients, so building good relationships is important. It's like making friends with people you meet on your journey. Happy clients can become repeat clients and even refer you to others.

Starting as a freelancer in online jobs is an exciting adventure where you get to showcase your skills and take control of your career. It's a journey that begins with self-discovery and gradually leads to success as you build your reputation and experience in the freelancing world.

Finding Freelance Opportunities

Finding freelance opportunities in online jobs is like searching for new adventures and challenges that match your skills and interests. It's a bit like being an explorer looking for hidden treasures. Here's how you can discover and pursue freelance work online:

1. Freelance Job Platforms and Websites:
Think of these platforms as marketplaccs where clients post job opportunities, and freelancers like you can apply. Popular platforms include Upwork, Freelancer, and Fiverr. You'll create a profile on these websites and search for jobs that match your skills.

2. Networking and Building Client Relationships:
Networking is like making friends in the world of freelancing. You can connect with people in your industry through social media, online

forums, and professional networks like LinkedIn. Building strong relationships can lead to referrals and more freelance work.

3. Marketing Your Freelance Services:

Imagine you're promoting a product. In freelancing, you're promoting your skills and services. You can create a personal website, use social media, and even run online ads to showcase what you can do.

4. Freelance Marketplaces in Niche Industries:

Some industries have specialized freelance marketplaces. For example, if you're a graphic designer, you might explore websites like 99designs or Behance. These platforms focus on specific niches and can be great for finding targeted opportunities.

5. Job Boards and Freelance Communities:

Job boards are like bulletin boards where clients post freelance gigs. Freelance communities are online groups of freelancers who share job leads and advice. Joining these communities can help you discover job opportunities and connect with experienced freelancers.

6. Pitching to Potential Clients:

Pitching is like making a persuasive offer. You can reach out directly to potential clients or companies that you'd like to work with. You'll craft a compelling pitch that explains how your skills can benefit them.

7. Online Market Research:

Just like researching a topic, you can research the market for your freelance services. You'll learn about your competition, understand client needs, and identify gaps where your skills can fill a demand.

8. Freelance Agencies and Intermediaries:

Some agencies act as intermediaries between clients and freelancers. They can help you find freelance work and handle administrative tasks like contracts and payments. This can be a convenient way to secure projects.

Finding freelance opportunities in online jobs is an ongoing journey. It's about being proactive, showcasing your skills, and connecting with the right clients or companies. As you explore different avenues, you'll discover exciting projects that align with your expertise and interests, helping you build a successful freelance career.

Managing Freelance Projects

Managing freelance projects in online jobs is like being the captain of your own ship. You're in charge of making sure your work gets done well and on time. Here's how you can successfully manage your freelance projects:

1. Negotiating Contracts and Setting Rates: Negotiating is like agreeing on the rules of your journey. When you start a project, you'll discuss the terms with your client. This includes the scope of work, deadlines, and how much you'll get paid.

2. Effective Project Management and Time Tracking:

Project management is like planning your route and keeping track of your progress. You'll use tools like calendars and project management software to organize tasks, set deadlines, and ensure you stay on schedule.

3. Handling Client Feedback and Revisions:

Just like listening to feedback from your travel companions, you'll listen to your client's feedback. Sometimes, they might ask for changes or revisions to your work. You'll need to be open to their suggestions and make improvements when needed.

4. Communication with Clients:

Communication is like having a compass that keeps you on the right path. You'll stay in touch with your clients regularly, providing updates on your progress and addressing any questions or concerns they have.

5. Meeting Deadlines:

Meeting deadlines is like reaching your destinations on time. It's important to stick to the agreed-upon schedule and deliver your work when promised. This builds trust with your clients.

6. Handling Multiple Projects:

Sometimes, you'll be juggling several projects at once. It's like managing multiple trips simultaneously. You'll need good organization skills to ensure that each project gets the attention it deserves.

7. Time Management:

Time management is like planning your day effectively. You'll allocate time for work, breaks, and personal activities. This helps you maintain a healthy work-life balance.

8. Invoicing and Payment:
Invoicing is like sending a bill for your services. You'll create invoices for your clients, specifying the work completed and the amount owed. Make sure to keep track of payments and follow up if necessary.

9. Contract Compliance:
Your contract is like a travel itinerary. It outlines the terms and conditions of your project. You'll ensure that both you and your client adhere to the contract throughout the project.

10. Client Relationships:
- Building strong client relationships is like making friends along your journey. Happy clients are more likely to hire you again or refer you to others, so maintaining a positive relationship is crucial.

Managing freelance projects is about being organized, communicating effectively, and delivering high-quality work. Just like a successful voyage, it requires careful planning and execution to ensure a smooth and satisfying journey in your freelance career.

Financial Aspects of Freelancing

Managing the financial aspects of freelancing in online jobs is like handling your own finances as you navigate through your professional journey. Here's a closer look at what this entails:

1. Managing Income, Expenses, and Taxes:
Think of your income as the money you earn from freelancing, and expenses as the costs associated with your work. You'll need to keep track of both. It's like balancing your income and spending in everyday life. Additionally, you'll need to understand and fulfill your tax obligations, just as you do with personal taxes.

2. Creating Invoices and Tracking Payments:
Invoices are like bills you send to clients for your services. You'll create professional invoices

that include details of the work completed and the amount owed. It's important to keep a record of these invoices and track when payments are due.

3. Setting Rates and Pricing:

Setting your rates is similar to deciding how much your services are worth. You'll consider factors like your skills, experience, market demand, and competition to determine your pricing. It's like determining the value of a product.

4. Budgeting and Financial Planning:

Budgeting is like planning your expenses for a trip. You'll create a financial plan that outlines how you'll allocate your earnings. This helps ensure you have enough money for both business and personal needs.

5. Financial Safety Nets:

Just as you might have savings for emergencies in your personal life, you'll need financial safety nets in freelancing. This could include setting aside a portion of your income for unexpected expenses or slow periods when you might not have as much work.

6. Retirement Planning:

Freelancers are responsible for their own retirement planning, much like planning for your retirement in traditional employment. You'll need to consider options like setting up retirement accounts or investments for your future financial security.

7. Managing Irregular Income:

Freelancers often have irregular income, which means your earnings may vary from month to month. It's like having a fluctuating income source. You'll need strategies to manage and budget for these income fluctuations.

8. Financial Tools and Software:

Just as you might use financial apps to manage your personal finances, freelancers often use accounting and financial software to streamline their financial tasks. These tools can help with invoicing, expense tracking, and financial reporting.

9. Emergency Fund and Insurance:
Having an emergency fund and considering insurance options is like preparing for unexpected events during your journey. These financial safety measures can provide a safety net in case of emergencies or unexpected situations.

Managing the financial aspects of freelancing is essential for maintaining financial stability and ensuring that you can enjoy the benefits of your online job while also securing your financial future. It's like being the captain of your financial ship as you sail through the world of freelancing.

Financial Aspects of Freelancing

Taking care of the financial aspects of freelancing in online jobs is like managing your own money as you navigate your career journey. Here's a closer look at what this means:

1. Managing Income, Expenses, and Taxes:
Your income is the money you earn from freelancing, while expenses are the costs related to your work, like software subscriptions or internet bills. Just like managing your household budget, you need to track your income and expenses. You'll also need to understand and pay taxes, similar to how you pay taxes on your personal income.

2. Creating Invoices and Tracking Payments:
Creating invoices is like sending bills to your clients. You'll make professional invoices that show the work you've done and how much you should be paid. Keeping track of these invoices and when payments are due is crucial.

3. Setting Rates and Pricing:
Setting your rates is similar to deciding how much your services are worth. You'll consider factors like your skills, experience, the demand

for your services, and what other freelancers charge. It's like pricing a product or service.

4. Budgeting and Financial Planning:
Budgeting is like planning how you'll spend your money. You'll create a budget that outlines your planned expenses, ensuring you allocate enough for both your business and personal needs.

5. Financial Safety Nets:
Having financial safety nets is like saving money for unexpected situations. Freelancers often set aside a portion of their income for emergencies or slower periods when they might not have as much work.

6. Retirement Planning:
Freelancers are responsible for their own retirement planning, similar to how people in traditional jobs plan for their retirement. You'll need to think about things like setting up retirement accounts or investments to secure your financial future.

7. Managing Irregular Income:

Freelancers often experience irregular income, meaning their earnings can vary from month to month. It's like having a job with a fluctuating paycheck. To manage this, you'll need strategies to handle and budget for these income fluctuations.

8. Financial Tools and Software:

Similar to using apps to track personal finances, freelancers often use accounting and financial software to simplify tasks. These tools help with invoicing, expense tracking, and financial reporting.

9. Emergency Fund and Insurance:

Having an emergency fund and considering insurance options is like preparing for unexpected events during your career journey. These financial safety measures can provide a financial cushion in case of emergencies or unforeseen situations.

Managing the financial aspects of freelancing is essential for financial stability and securing your future. It's like taking control of your financial ship as you sail through the world of freelancing.

Balancing Freelance Work and Personal Life

Balancing freelance work and personal life in online jobs is like keeping a good balance between your job and your personal time. It's a bit like making sure you have time for both schoolwork and fun when you're a student. Here's how you can do it:

1. Time Management: Time management is like creating a schedule. You decide when you'll work and when you'll have time for yourself and your loved ones. This way, you make sure you have time for everything.

2. Setting Boundaries: Setting boundaries is like creating rules. You tell yourself and your clients when your work hours are, and when you're off the clock. It's important not to let work take over all your free time.

3. Taking Breaks: Taking breaks is like having recess during school. You pause your work to relax and recharge. Short breaks during the day can help you stay fresh and focused.

4. Prioritizing Tasks: Prioritizing tasks is like deciding which homework to do first. You figure out which work tasks are most important and do them before less urgent ones.

5. Communication: Communication is like talking to your friends or teachers. If you need some time off or have personal commitments, you let your clients or colleagues know in advance. Good communication helps everyone understand your schedule.

6. Avoiding Overwork: Overworking is like studying too much and missing out on playtime.

It can lead to feeling exhausted and stressed. Stick to your work hours to avoid burnout.

7. Enjoying Personal Activities: Just like enjoying your hobbies or having playtime, make sure you have time for activities you love. Whether it's reading, exercising, spending time with family, or pursuing your interests, personal activities are essential for your well-being.

8. Unplugging from Technology: Unplugging is like turning off the TV or video games when it's time to focus. Take breaks from screens to relax and reduce stress.

9. Self-Care: Self-care is like taking care of your health. Get enough sleep, eat well, and exercise regularly. A healthy body and mind help you maintain balance.

10. Flexibility: Flexibility is like being open to changes. Sometimes, unexpected things happen, and you might need to adjust your plans. Being adaptable helps you manage your time effectively.

Balancing freelance work and personal life is about making sure you don't spend all your time working. It's important to have time for yourself, your family, and the things that bring you happiness. Just like a balanced scale, finding the right equilibrium between work and personal life is essential for a satisfying and joyful freelance career.

Building a Freelance Portfolio

Building a freelance portfolio in online jobs is like creating a showcase of your best work to prove your skills and attract potential clients. Imagine it as putting together a collection of your favorite drawings or crafts to show to others. Here's how you can do it:

1. Select Your Best Work: Just like picking your favorite drawings, you choose the work that represents your skills the best. This could be articles you've written, designs you've created, or projects you've completed.

2. Create a Digital Portfolio: Your digital portfolio is like a photo album online. You'll put your selected work on a website or platform designed for showcasing your talents. It's where potential clients can see what you can do.

3. Organize Your Projects: Organizing your portfolio is like arranging your artwork neatly. You'll group your projects by type or category, making it easy for visitors to find what interests them.

4. Provide Descriptions: Descriptions are like captions for your drawings. You'll explain each project, what you did, and the skills you used. This helps clients understand your work better.

5. Show Your Progress: Just like showing how you improved your art over time, you can include older projects and newer ones to demonstrate your growth and development.

6. Keep it Updated: Updating your portfolio is like adding new drawings to your collection. When you complete new projects, make sure to add them to your portfolio to keep it fresh and relevant.

7. Share Your Portfolio: Sharing your portfolio is like displaying your art in an art gallery. You'll share the link to your portfolio with potential clients or include it in your job applications.

8. Gather Testimonials: Testimonials are like getting compliments on your art. When clients are happy with your work, ask them for a short recommendation. Positive feedback adds credibility to your portfolio.

9. Seek Feedback: Just like asking others what they think of your art, you can ask peers or mentors for feedback on your portfolio. They can offer suggestions for improvement.

10. Be Proud of Your Work: Lastly, be proud of your portfolio, just like you're proud of your artwork. It represents your skills and creativity, and it's a valuable tool for landing freelance gigs.

Building a freelance portfolio is a way to showcase your talents and prove to potential clients that you're the right person for the job. It's like sharing your art with the world and finding people who appreciate your creativity and skills.

Legal and Contractual Considerations

Understanding legal and contractual considerations in online jobs is like knowing the rules of the game before you start playing. It's important to protect yourself and your work. Here's how to navigate these aspects:

1. Contracts Are Like Agreements: Contracts are formal agreements between you and your client. They outline what you'll do, how much you'll get paid, and when the work should be finished. Just like agreeing on the rules of a game, contracts ensure everyone is on the same page.

2. Read Before You Sign: Reading contracts carefully is like reading the game instructions before you play. Make sure you understand all the terms and conditions. If something doesn't seem right, ask questions or seek legal advice.

3. Payment Terms Are Like Scoring Rules: Payment terms are like the rules for scoring points in a game. Contracts specify when and how you'll get paid. Some clients pay upfront, while others pay after the work is done. Make sure these terms are clear.

4. Protecting Your Work: Protecting your work is like safeguarding your game pieces. Contracts may include clauses about who owns the rights to your work. Ensure you retain ownership or get paid for transferring those rights.

5. Dispute Resolution is Like Refereeing: Just as referees resolve conflicts in a game, contracts often have clauses about dispute resolution. This outlines how disagreements between you and your client will be resolved, such as through arbitration or mediation.

6. Copyright and Intellectual Property: Copyright and intellectual property rights are like the ownership of game rules. Make sure your contract addresses who owns the rights to your work. This is crucial, especially if you're creating content, designs, or code.

7. Taxes and Reporting: Taxes are like keeping score of your earnings. Freelancers often need to report their income and pay taxes. Understand your tax obligations in your location and keep records of your earnings and expenses.

8. Non-Disclosure Agreements (NDAs): NDAs are like secret moves in a game. Some clients may require you to sign an NDA, which means you can't share confidential information about their project. Make sure you're comfortable with the terms before signing.

9. Compliance with Laws: Complying with laws is like following the game rules. Ensure your freelance work aligns with local, state, and federal laws. This includes business licenses, permits, and any industry-specific regulations.

10. Seek Legal Advice When Needed: Just as you might ask for help from a coach in a game, seek legal advice if you're unsure about any contract terms or legal matters. An attorney can help protect your interests.

Understanding legal and contractual considerations is like understanding the rules of the road. It helps you navigate the freelance world safely and ensures that both you and your clients are treated fairly.

Specialized Freelance Niches

Exploring specialized freelance niches in online jobs is like discovering unique fields where you can apply your skills and expertise. It's a bit like finding hidden treasures in the world of freelancing. Let's take a closer look:

1. What Are Specialized Niches? Specialized niches are like specific playgrounds within the larger freelancing world. They are areas where you can offer your services and expertise to a highly targeted audience.

2. Identifying Your Niche: Identifying your niche is like discovering your superpower. You figure out what you're exceptionally good at and passionate about. It could be writing about technology, designing wedding invitations, or coding mobile apps.

3. Finding Your Target Audience: Finding your target audience is like knowing who will enjoy playing a particular game. You identify the people or businesses that need your specialized skills and services.

4. Building Expertise: Building expertise in your niche is like becoming a master at a particular game. You continuously improve your skills and knowledge to stand out in your chosen field.

5. Networking in Your Niche: Networking in your niche is like making friends who share your gaming interests. You connect with others in your specialized field, which can lead to collaboration and new opportunities.

6. Showcasing Your Work: Showcasing your work is like displaying your game achievements. You create a portfolio or showcase your projects that demonstrate your skills and expertise in your niche.

7. Setting Competitive Rates: Setting competitive rates is like pricing your game tokens. You determine how much you'll charge for your services, considering factors like your expertise and the demand in your niche.

8. Marketing Yourself: Marketing yourself is like promoting a game. You use various strategies to let potential clients know about your services, such as having a professional website or using social media.

9. Staying Updated: Staying updated is like keeping up with the latest game trends. In specialized niches, you need to stay informed about industry developments and changes to remain competitive.

10. Embracing Challenges: - Embracing challenges in your niche is like taking on tough levels in a game. You may face unique hurdles, but overcoming them can lead to greater success.

11. Seeking Niche-Specific Opportunities: Seeking niche-specific opportunities is like looking for rare collectibles in a game. You actively search for projects and clients that align with your specialized skills and interests.

12. Growing Your Reputation: Growing your reputation in your niche is like earning a prestigious title in a game. As you deliver high-quality work and build a positive reputation, more clients in your niche will seek your services.

Exploring specialized freelance niches allows you to carve out a unique path in the freelancing world. It's about finding your own corner of expertise, much like discovering a special adventure within a larger gaming universe.

Freelancing in the Gig Economy

Freelancing in the gig economy while working online is a bit like being a player in a video game where you complete various quests or tasks to earn rewards. In freelancing, these quests are the jobs or "gigs" you take on. Here's a closer look at freelancing in the gig economy:

1. What Is the Gig Economy? The gig economy is like a marketplace where people offer their skills and services as independent workers rather than traditional employees. It's a world where you can choose different "gigs" to work on, just like selecting different quests in a game.

2. Flexibility and Variety: Freelancing in the gig economy offers flexibility, much like choosing which quests to complete in a game. You decide when and where you work, and you can take on a variety of projects that interest you.

3. Gig Platforms: Gig platforms are like the central hub where you find quests in a game.

These are websites or apps where you can discover and apply for freelance jobs. Examples include Upwork, Fiverr, and TaskRabbit.

4. Freelance Skills: Freelance skills are your abilities, much like the skills and talents of your character in a game. These can include writing, graphic design, coding, social media management, and many more.

5. Bidding and Proposals: Bidding on gigs is like offering your services for a particular quest. You submit proposals to potential clients, explaining how you'll complete their project and how much you'll charge.

6. Project-Based Work: Freelance work is often project-based, similar to completing a level in a game. You work on specific tasks or assignments, and once they're done, you move on to the next project.

7. Building a Reputation: Building a reputation is like leveling up in a game. As you successfully complete gigs and receive positive feedback from clients, your reputation as a skilled freelancer grows.

8. Managing Your Business: Managing your freelance business is akin to managing resources in a game. You handle tasks like invoicing, tracking expenses, and ensuring you have the tools and skills needed to complete gigs.

9. Income Variability: Income in the gig economy can vary, much like the rewards you earn in different quests. Some gigs pay more than others, and your income may fluctuate from month to month.

10. Networking and Growth: - Networking in the gig economy is like forming alliances with other players in a game. You can connect with other freelancers, collaborate on projects, and learn from one another to grow your skills and opportunities.

11. Challenges and Rewards: - Freelancing in the gig economy presents challenges, similar to facing obstacles in a game. However, overcoming these challenges can lead to rewards such as financial independence and a fulfilling career.

12. Adapting to Change: - Adapting to change is like adjusting your strategy in a game when you encounter new challenges. The gig economy is constantly evolving, so staying adaptable is crucial for long-term success.

Freelancing in the gig economy offers a dynamic and flexible way to work online, where you can choose your quests and build your career according to your interests and skills. It's like embarking on a journey through a digital realm where your abilities and efforts determine your success.

CHAPTER 4
THE POWER AND FREEDOM OF WORKING REMOTELY

Remote employment in online jobs is like having a job where you don't have to be in a specific office or location to work. It's a bit like playing a multiplayer online game with friends from different parts of the world.

The Rise of Remote Work

The rise of remote work in online jobs is like a big shift in how people do their jobs. It's a bit like when a new game becomes incredibly popular and everyone wants to play it. Here's what's happening:

1. Changing Work Landscape: The rise of remote work means that more and more people are doing their jobs from places other than traditional offices. Instead of going to a physical workplace, they're working from home, cafes, or even while traveling.

2. Technology Makes it Possible: Technology, like the internet and video conferencing, is like the magic that makes remote work happen. It allows people to connect, communicate, and get work done from anywhere in the world.

3. Flexibility and Freedom: Remote work offers flexibility, which is a bit like choosing when and how to play a game. It lets employees set their own schedules and work in ways that suit them, giving them more freedom.

4. Benefits for Employers: Employers are also benefiting from remote work. They can tap into a global talent pool and often save on office space and other overhead costs.

5. Work-Life Balance: People are finding better work-life balance with remote work. It's like having more time to spend with family, pursue hobbies, or just relax because they don't have to commute.

6. Increased Productivity: Some remote workers say they're more productive because they can choose their work environment, whether it's a quiet home office or a cozy corner in a cafe.

7. Job Opportunities Everywhere: The rise of remote work means that job opportunities are no longer limited to a specific city or location. It's like being able to play your favorite game with friends from all over the world.

8. Challenges to Overcome: However, remote work isn't without its challenges. It can be lonely at times, and communication can be trickier when you're not in the same place as your colleagues.

9. Future of Work: Many experts believe that remote work is here to stay and will continue to shape the future of work. It's like a new game that's become a permanent part of the gaming world.

10. Opportunities for All:- The rise of remote work is creating opportunities for people of all backgrounds and abilities. It's like opening up the game to players of all skill levels.

The rise of remote work is changing how people approach their jobs, offering more flexibility and freedom. It's like a new way to play the game of work, allowing individuals to find a balance that suits their lives and preferences.

Advantages of Remote Employment

The advantages of remote employment in online jobs are like the good things that come with playing your favorite game. It's a bit like discovering hidden treasures that make the game more enjoyable. Here are some of the key advantages:

1. Flexibility in Where You Work: Remote employment allows you to work from different locations, such as your home, a coffee shop, or even a beach if you like. It's like choosing your favorite game level.

2. Improved Work-Life Balance: Remote work can help you balance your job with personal life. It's a bit like having more time to spend with family, pursue hobbies, or simply relax because you don't have to commute.

3. Customizable Work Environment: You can create your ideal work environment. Whether you prefer a quiet home office or the buzz of a café, it's like setting up your game station just the way you like it.

4. Reduced Commuting Stress: Remote employment eliminates the need for a daily commute. This means less time stuck in traffic or crowded trains and more time for other activities.

5. Access to a Global Job Market: You can work for companies or clients from different parts of the world. It's like playing a game with friends from all over the globe, bringing diversity to your work experience.

6. Increased Job Opportunities: Remote work opens up job opportunities that may not be available locally. You can find roles that match your skills and interests, just like choosing your favorite character in a game.

7. Cost Savings: Working remotely can lead to cost savings. You'll spend less on commuting, work attire, and meals, allowing you to keep more of your hard-earned money.

8. Enhanced Productivity: Some remote workers find they're more productive because they have control over their work environment.

It's like being in charge of the game and making it work for you.

9. Health Benefits: Remote employment can lead to improved health. With more time for exercise and less exposure to commuting stress, you can focus on staying fit and healthy.

10. Job Security and Opportunities for All:- Remote work is often more inclusive, offering job opportunities to people with various abilities and backgrounds. It's like making the game accessible to all players.

11. Environmental Impact:- By reducing commuting, remote work can also have a positive impact on the environment by lowering carbon emissions.

12. Learning and Growth:- Remote work often involves using various digital tools and technologies, allowing you to learn and adapt to new skills and trends, similar to leveling up in a game.

Overall, the advantages of remote employment make it a rewarding and flexible option for many people. It's like finding power-ups and shortcuts in your favorite game, making your work-life experience more enjoyable and fulfilling.

Types of Remote Jobs

Remote jobs in online work are like different characters or roles you can choose in a game. Each type of job offers unique experiences and opportunities. Here are some common types of remote jobs:

1. Freelancing: Freelancers are like adventurers who take on quests (projects) for clients. They can be writers, designers, programmers, or marketers. Freelancing allows you to work on various projects for different clients.

2. Full-Time Remote Employment: Full-time remote employees are like dedicated players in a game. They work for a single company but do their job from home or another remote location. This setup provides job security and a steady income.

3. Remote Customer Service: Remote customer service agents are like customer support heroes. They help customers with inquiries, issues, and complaints via phone, email, or chat while working from home.

4. Virtual Assistants: Virtual assistants are like supportive sidekicks in a game. They provide administrative and organizational support to businesses and individuals. Tasks can include email management, scheduling, and research.

5. Online Teaching and Tutoring: Online teachers and tutors are like mentors who guide players through a game. They educate students in various subjects, languages, or skills through virtual classrooms and video conferencing.

6. Remote Software Development: Remote software developers are like coding wizards. They create and maintain software applications, websites, and systems from anywhere with an internet connection.

7. Digital Marketing and Social Media Management: Digital marketers and social media managers are like strategists who promote games to a wider audience. They handle online marketing campaigns, SEO, content creation, and social media presence for businesses.

8. Content Creation and Blogging: Content creators and bloggers are like storytellers who share their adventures. They write articles, create videos, or design graphics for websites, blogs, or social media channels.

9. Data Entry and Online Surveys: Data entry workers are like meticulous record keepers. They input data into databases, spreadsheets, or online forms. Some individuals participate in online surveys and earn rewards.

10. Remote Sales and Business Development:- Sales and business development professionals are like negotiators in a game. They build relationships with clients and seek new opportunities for their companies, all while working remotely.

11. Project Management:- Remote project managers are like team leaders who coordinate missions in a game. They plan, execute, and oversee projects, ensuring they are completed on time and within budget.

12. Remote Healthcare and Telemedicine:- Remote healthcare providers are like virtual doctors and nurses. They offer medical consultations, diagnoses, and treatment recommendations through video conferencing and telemedicine platforms.

These are just a few examples of the many remote job opportunities available. Much like choosing a character in a game, individuals can select the type of remote job that aligns with their skills, interests, and career goals in the online work world.

Remote Work Tools and Technology

Remote work in online jobs relies on special tools and technology that are a bit like the equipment and gadgets you use in a video game. These tools help you connect, communicate, and get your job done from anywhere. Here's a closer look:

1. Laptop or Computer: Your computer is like your game console. It's your main tool for working remotely. You use it to access the internet, run software, and communicate with others.

2. Internet Connection: An internet connection is like the electricity that powers your game console. Without it, remote work wouldn't be possible. It allows you to send emails, join video meetings, and access online resources.

3. Video Conferencing Software: Video conferencing software is like a magic portal that lets you see and talk to your colleagues or clients. It's used for virtual meetings, discussions, and presentations. Tools like Zoom, Microsoft Teams, and Skype are examples.

4. Email and Messaging Apps: These are like sending in-game messages to your team. Email and messaging apps like Gmail, Slack, and Microsoft Outlook help you stay in touch, share updates, and collaborate on projects.

5. Project Management Tools: Project management tools are like your quest log in a game. They help you keep track of tasks, deadlines, and progress. Tools like Trello, Asana, and Monday.com assist in organizing and managing projects.

6. Cloud Storage: Cloud storage is like a treasure chest where you store your work. It allows you to save and access files, documents, and data from anywhere. Popular services include Google Drive, Dropbox, and Microsoft OneDrive.

7. Collaborative Documents: Collaborative documents are like a shared game world where multiple players can edit at once. Tools like Google Docs and Microsoft Office Online enable real-time collaboration on documents, spreadsheets, and presentations.

8. Remote Desktop Software: Remote desktop software is like a portal that connects you to your work computer from afar. It's handy when you need to access files or applications on your office computer while working remotely.

9. Password Managers: Password managers are like shields protecting your login information. They help you securely store and manage passwords for various accounts, ensuring online safety.

10. Virtual Private Networks (VPNs):- VPNs are like invisibility cloaks that keep your online activities private and secure. They are crucial when working on sensitive tasks or accessing company networks remotely.

11. Headsets and Webcams:- These are like your communication gear in a game. Headsets with microphones and webcams help you participate in video conferences and meetings with clear audio and video.

12. Time Tracking Software:- Time tracking software is like a stopwatch for your work tasks. It helps you monitor how much time you spend on different activities and projects, ensuring efficient use of your work hours.

These tools and technology make remote work possible and efficient in online jobs. They're your allies in the virtual work world, ensuring you can collaborate, communicate, and complete tasks seamlessly, no matter where you are.

Remote Work Best Practices

Remote work in online jobs is like playing a game where you need to follow certain rules and strategies to succeed. Here are some best practices to make your remote work experience smooth and successful:

1. Set Up a Dedicated Workspace: Create a quiet and comfortable workspace at home or wherever you choose to work. It's like having your own gaming area with all your tools and equipment ready.

2. Stick to a Schedule: Establish a daily routine and stick to it. Set specific working hours to help you stay focused and organized, just like having a gaming schedule.

3. Dress for Success: While you don't need to wear a suit, dressing up a bit can put you in the right mindset for work. It's like choosing the right outfit for your in-game character.

4. Use Technology Wisely: Make sure your internet connection and remote work tools are reliable. It's like ensuring your game console and controllers are in good condition.

5. Communicate Effectively: Stay in touch with your team and clients through video meetings, chats, and emails Clear communication is crucial, much like coordinating with teammates in a game.

6. Set Clear Goals and Priorities: Define your daily tasks and prioritize them. It's like setting your objectives and missions in a game to know what to focus on first.

7. Take Regular Breaks: Just as you pause your game to recharge, take short breaks during work.

Stretch, walk around, or do something you enjoy to stay refreshed.

8. Avoid Multitasking: Focus on one task at a time. Multitasking can be distracting and reduce your productivity, similar to trying to play multiple games simultaneously.

9. Manage Distractions: Minimize distractions in your workspace. Turn off non-work-related notifications and let others in your household know when you're working.

10. Stay Organized:- Use project management tools and to-do lists to keep track of tasks and deadlines. It's like having a quest log in your game to keep track of your missions.

11. Seek Support and Clarification:- If you're unsure about something, don't hesitate to ask for help or clarification. It's like reaching out to fellow gamers or consulting game guides for advice.

12. Practice Self-Care:- Take care of your physical and mental well-being. Get enough sleep, eat healthily, and engage in activities you enjoy outside of work.

13. Celebrate Achievements:- Acknowledge your accomplishments and milestones. It's like celebrating your victories and leveling up in a game.

14. Learn Continuously:- Stay updated on industry trends and improve your skills. It's like acquiring new abilities and strategies as you progress in a game.

15. Disconnect After Work:- When your workday is over, disconnect from work-related tasks and enjoy your personal time. It's like saving your progress and turning off your game console.

Following these best practices can help you thrive in remote work and enjoy a successful online job experience, much like mastering the strategies and techniques in your favorite video game.

Remote Job Search and Freelancing Platforms

When you're looking for remote work or freelancing opportunities in online jobs, it's a bit like searching for the best games to play. There are specific websites and platforms designed to help you find these opportunities. Here's how it works:

1. Job Search Platforms: Job search platforms are like giant libraries filled with job listings. Websites like Indeed, LinkedIn, and Glassdoor list remote job openings from various companies. You can search for jobs by keywords, location, or industry, just as you might search for your favorite game.

2. Freelancing Platforms: Freelancing platforms are like marketplaces where you can offer your skills and services to potential clients. Websites such as Upwork, Fiverr, and Freelancer allow you to create profiles, showcase your talents, and bid on freelance projects, much like setting up your in-game character and choosing quests.

3. Remote Job Boards: Remote job boards are specialized websites that focus solely on remote job listings. Websites like Remote.co and We Work Remotely curate remote job opportunities across various industries, making it easier to find the perfect match.

4. Company Career Pages: Many companies have dedicated career pages on their websites where they list remote job openings. It's like visiting a game developer's official website to learn about their latest releases and job openings.

5. Networking Sites: Professional networking sites like LinkedIn are like virtual meeting places for job seekers and recruiters. You can connect with potential employers and join groups related to your field, similar to joining a gaming community.

6. Niche Job Boards: Some industries have niche job boards tailored to specific professions. For example, the ProBlogger job board is ideal for remote writers and bloggers, much like finding a gaming forum focused on your favorite game genre.

7. Freelancer Communities: Online freelancer communities, such as Reddit's /r/freelance, are like guilds of experienced freelancers. You can seek advice, share experiences, and learn from others in the freelance world.

8. Skill-Specific Platforms: Some platforms cater to specific skills or industries. For instance, GitHub is a hub for software developers, while Behance is a showcase for creative professionals. It's like exploring dedicated gaming forums for fans of a particular game genre.

9. Global Marketplaces: Global freelance marketplaces, like Toptal and Guru, connect businesses with top talent worldwide. These platforms offer a wide range of projects and opportunities, similar to exploring diverse game worlds.

10. Remote Job Aggregators:- Remote job aggregators, such as Remote OK and FlexJobs, compile remote job listings from various sources into one convenient location. It's like having a gaming dashboard that displays all your favorite games in one place.

11. Application and Proposal Submissions:- To apply for remote jobs or freelance projects, you typically need to submit your resume, cover letter, and portfolio, much like presenting your gaming achievements and skills to gain entry into a gaming guild.

12. Interviews and Negotiations:- If a company or client is interested in your profile, they may invite you for an interview or negotiation. It's like participating in discussions with fellow players or game developers to plan your next move.

By exploring these platforms and using them effectively, you can find remote work and freelancing opportunities that align with your skills and interests, just as you discover new and exciting games to play.

Remote Work Trends and the Future

Remote work trends in online jobs are a bit like predicting the future of a game—it's exciting and constantly evolving. Here's a look at what the future may hold for remote work:

1. Hybrid Work Models: Many companies are likely to adopt hybrid work models, allowing employees to split their time between working remotely and in the office. It's like having a mix of single-player and multiplayer game modes.

2. Global Talent Pools: The future may see companies tapping into global talent pools, hiring remote workers from around the world. It's like forming international teams in a multiplayer game.

3. Flexible Schedules: Remote work will likely offer even more flexibility in terms of working hours. You may have the freedom to choose when you work, similar to playing a game at your own pace.

4. Digital Nomadism: Digital nomadism, where individuals work while traveling, may become more common. It's like embarking on an adventure in different game worlds while still progressing in your quest.

5. Improved Technology: Technology will continue to advance, offering better tools for remote work. Enhanced virtual reality and augmented reality may change the way we collaborate, making it feel like working together in a game.

6. Emphasis on Wellbeing: Companies will likely focus more on employee wellbeing, offering mental health support and wellness programs. It's like replenishing your character's health and stamina in a game to perform at your best.

7. Inclusivity and Accessibility: Remote work may become even more inclusive, offering opportunities to individuals with disabilities. It's like making sure that everyone can enjoy playing the game, regardless of their abilities.

8. Cybersecurity and Data Protection: As remote work grows, so does the need for cybersecurity and data protection. Companies will invest in secure systems to protect sensitive information, similar to guarding valuable in-game assets.

9. Upskilling and Reskilling: Continuous learning and upskilling will be essential for staying competitive in remote work. It's like acquiring new skills and abilities as you progress in a game.

10. Environmental Considerations:- Remote work may have a positive impact on the environment by reducing commuting and office space requirements. It's like playing a game with eco-friendly gameplay mechanics.

11. Regulatory Changes:- Governments may introduce new regulations and policies related to remote work, ensuring fair labor practices and tax considerations. It's like adjusting the rules of the game to maintain fairness.

12. Work-Life Integration:- The line between work and personal life may blur even further, emphasizing work-life integration rather than separation. It's like seamlessly switching between game and real life.

13. Emerging Industries:- New industries and job roles related to remote work may emerge, much like discovering hidden levels or expansion packs in a game.

14. Improved Collaboration Tools:- Collaboration tools will continue to evolve, making it easier for remote teams to work together effectively, much like having advanced communication tools in a game to coordinate with teammates.

15. Embracing Change:- Remote workers will need to adapt to change and stay open to new technologies and work processes, similar to leveling up and acquiring new strategies in a game.

The future of remote work in online jobs is full of possibilities, and staying informed and adaptable will be key to thriving in this dynamic landscape, much like progressing through different levels and challenges in a game.

Remote Work Trends and the Future

Thinking about remote work trends and the future in online jobs is a bit like imagining what the next big adventure in your favorite video game will be. Here's a look at what's coming:

1. Hybrid Work Models: In the future, we might see a mix of remote and in-office work. It's like having both solo and multiplayer modes in a game.

2. Global Talent Pool: Companies may hire people from anywhere globally. It's like forming a team of players from different parts of the world to tackle in-game challenges.

3. Flexibility in Schedules: The future could offer even more flexibility in when you work.

It's like choosing when to embark on quests in your game.

4. Digital Nomads: Some folks may work while traveling, known as digital nomadism. It's like exploring various gaming worlds while still progressing in your adventures.

5. Better Technology: As technology improves, we may have cooler tools for remote work, perhaps even virtual reality and augmented reality for a more immersive experience, like being inside a game.

6. Wellbeing Matters: Companies might focus more on keeping employees happy and healthy, like making sure your in-game character is in top shape.

7. Inclusivity and Access: The future might make remote work more accessible for people with disabilities, ensuring everyone can join the game.

8. Cybersecurity: With remote work growing, cybersecurity will be a top concern. It's like protecting precious items in your game from thieves.

9. Learning Never Stops: Continuous learning will be crucial to stay competitive, much like acquiring new skills in your game as you level up.

10. Environmentally Friendly:- Remote work can be kinder to the environment by reducing commuting and office space needs, like playing a game with eco-friendly features.

11. Government Rules:- Governments may introduce new rules for remote work to ensure fairness and taxes. It's like changing the rules of your game for balance.

12. Work-Life Blend:- Instead of a strict work-life balance, we might embrace a blend of the two, like switching between real life and the game seamlessly.

13. New Industries:- New industries and job roles related to remote work may emerge, just as you discover new quests and challenges in your game.

14. Better Collaboration Tools:- Tools for remote teamwork will get even better, like having advanced communication tools to strategize with fellow players.

15. Embracing Change:- To succeed, we'll need to adapt to new tech and work ways, much like learning new tactics and strategies in your game.

The future of remote work in online jobs is like an uncharted territory in a game, full of exciting quests and surprises. Being ready to learn, adapt, and explore this evolving landscape will be key to your success, just as it is in your favorite video game.

CHAPTER 5

THE ROAD TO ONLINE ENTREPRENEURIAL SUCCESS

Imagine that online entrepreneurial success is like embarking on a thrilling quest in an online game. To reach your destination, you need to follow a path paved with various steps and challenges. Here's an overview of what this road looks like:

Nurturing Your Business Idea

Imagine nurturing your business idea is like taking care of a plant in a game. Your idea is like a seed that has the potential to grow into something big and exciting. Here's how you can do it:

1. Seed of Inspiration: Every great business idea starts with inspiration. It's like finding a hidden treasure chest in the game. Look for problems that need solving or opportunities to make people's lives better.

2. Research and Exploration: Before planting your idea, explore the landscape. It's like exploring different game levels to understand what challenges and competitors you might face.

3. Idea Refinement: Just as you sharpen your sword in the game, refine your idea. Make it clear and unique. Think about how it can stand out in the market.

4. Target Audience Identification: Identify who your customers will be. It's like knowing your target enemy's weaknesses in the game. Understand their needs, desires, and problems your idea can solve.

5. Testing the Waters: Before going all in, test your idea. It's like trying out a new strategy in the game. Start small, gather feedback, and see how it performs.

6. Growth Strategy: Plan how your idea can grow. Just as your character levels up, think about how your business can expand, attract more customers, and generate income.

7. Risk Assessment: Every game has risks, and so does business. Think about potential obstacles and how you can overcome them. It's like preparing for tough challenges in the game.

8. Feeding Your Idea: Like a plant needs water and sunlight, your idea needs resources and attention. Invest time, effort, and possibly some money to nurture its growth.

9. Monitoring Progress: Keep an eye on how your idea is growing. Track key indicators, just as you track your character's progress in the game.

10. Adaptability:- Sometimes, you need to change your strategy in the game. Likewise, be open to adjusting your business idea based on what you learn and how the market evolves.

Nurturing your business idea is like tending to a precious in-game asset. With care, attention, and the right strategy, your idea can grow into a successful online business.

Creating a Solid Business Plan

Think of creating a business plan like drawing a map for your online job adventure. It helps you know where you're going and how to get there. Here's how to create a solid business plan:

1. The Starting Point: Begin by understanding where you are now, just like locating your character's starting point in a game. What skills, resources, and knowledge do you have?

2. The Destination: Define your goal, like reaching a specific level or defeating a big boss in a game. What do you want to achieve with your online job?

3. Strategy Building: Develop a strategy, like planning your moves in a game. How will you reach your goal? What steps will you take?

4. Know Your Market: Research your target market, similar to understanding your game environment. Who are your customers, and what do they need?

5. Competitor Analysis: Study your competitors, just as you'd study your gaming rivals. What are others in your field doing, and how can you do it better?

6. Product or Service Details: Describe what you're offering, like explaining your character's abilities in the game. What value does your online job bring to customers?

7. Marketing Plan: Plan how you'll tell people about your online job, like planning your quest in the game. What marketing strategies will you use?

8. Financial Projections: Estimate your income and expenses, like managing your in-game resources. How much money do you expect to make, and how much will you spend?

9. Resource Needs: List what you need to make your online job work, like gathering the right tools and equipment in the game. Do you need a website, software, or support?

10. Risk Assessment:- Think about potential challenges and how you'll deal with them, just as you prepare for tough game levels. What could go wrong, and how can you overcome it?

11. Timelines and Milestones:- Set deadlines and milestones, like planning when to complete game missions. When will you achieve certain goals in your online job?

12. Team and Roles:- If you have a team, assign roles and responsibilities, much like forming a party with different characters in a game. Who does what to make your plan work?

13. Review and Adjust:- Regularly review your plan and make adjustments, similar to adapting your gaming strategy when things change.

14. Budget:- Create a budget, like managing your in-game currency. How much will you spend on different aspects of your online job?

15. Legal and Compliance:- Ensure you follow the rules and regulations, like staying within the game's guidelines. Are there legal requirements for your online job?

16. Presentation:- Finally, present your plan clearly, like sharing your gaming strategy with teammates. Your plan should be easy for others to understand.

Creating a solid business plan is like preparing for a grand quest in your favorite game. It helps you stay focused, make informed decisions, and increase your chances of success in the world of online jobs.

Market Research and Analysis

Imagine market research and analysis as your tool to uncover hidden treasures in the world of online jobs. Here's how it works:

1. Discovering Your Battlefield: Just as you explore different game environments, start by identifying the market for your online job. Who are your potential customers? Where are they?

2. Understanding Your Opponents: Think of your competitors as fellow gamers in the same arena. Study them to see what they offer and how they attract customers.

3. Identifying Market Trends: Keep an eye on trends in the online job world, similar to watching for updates and changes in your favorite game. What skills or services are in demand right now?

4. Customer Needs and Desires: Understand what your customers want, much like figuring out what quests or missions your fellow players enjoy. What problems can your online job solve for them?

5. Pricing Strategies: Determine how much you can charge for your online job, just like setting a fair price for items in a game's marketplace.

6. Market Size and Growth: Analyze the size of your potential market and its growth rate, similar to assessing the popularity of different game levels.

7. Demographics and Psychographics: Learn about your customers' demographics (age, location, gender) and psychographics (interests, behaviors), like understanding the characteristics of different game characters.

8. Market Segmentation: Divide your market into segments, similar to creating different gaming zones. This helps you tailor your online job to specific customer groups.

9. SWOT Analysis: Like a character's strengths and weaknesses in a game, analyze your online job's strengths, weaknesses, opportunities, and threats.

10. Customer Feedback:- Listen to your customers' feedback, similar to paying attention to player reviews and comments in the gaming community.

11. Market Entry Points:- Identify where and how you can enter the market, much like choosing the best entry point in a game level.

12. Market Research Tools:- Use online tools and resources to gather data, like using in-game guides or walkthroughs to navigate challenges.

13. Adjusting Your Strategy:- If the market changes, adapt your strategy, just as you'd change your tactics in the game when facing different foes.

14. Competitive Advantage:- Find ways to stand out from your competitors, like using unique strategies or abilities in the game to win battles.

15. Market Validation:- Before going all-in, validate your market research findings by testing your online job with a smaller audience, similar to completing a mini-quest before tackling the main mission.

16. Continual Monitoring:- Keep monitoring the market, just as you explore new game levels and challenges. Stay updated to remain competitive.

Market research and analysis are like equipping yourself with a treasure map in the world of online jobs. They guide you toward the best opportunities and help you make wise decisions to succeed in your online job venture.

Product or Service Development

Picture product or service development as creating a magical item or a powerful spell in a game. Here's how it works in online jobs:

1. Idea Generation: Just like inventing a new magic spell, it starts with brainstorming ideas for your product or service. What can you offer that's unique or valuable?

2. Concept Design: Imagine sketching out the details of your magic spell. Design your product or service, considering how it will benefit your customers.

3. Research and Planning: Similar to gathering ingredients for a spell, research what's needed to create your product or deliver your service. Plan the steps.

4. Prototyping: Build a prototype or a test version of your product, much like experimenting with a new spell to see if it works.

5. Testing and Feedback: Test your prototype on a small scale, like trying out your spell on a minor challenge. Gather feedback from early users or customers.

6. Refinement: Based on feedback, refine your product or service, making it more powerful and effective, like perfecting your spell.

7. Quality Assurance: Ensure your product or service works flawlessly, just as you'd ensure your spell doesn't have unintended side effects.

8. Cost Estimation: Calculate the cost of producing your product or delivering your service, similar to the cost of gathering spell ingredients.

9. Pricing Strategy:- Decide how much to charge for your product or service, considering what customers are willing to pay.

10. Scalability:- Think about how easily you can produce more units of your product or deliver your service if there's high demand.

11. Legal Considerations:- Ensure you're following laws and regulations related to your product or service, like adhering to rules in the game world.

12. Production and Delivery:- Finally, produce your product or start delivering your service to customers, similar to using your spell in different situations.

13. Customer Support:- Provide customer support, just as you'd assist fellow players with questions or issues in the game.

14. Feedback Loop:- Continuously gather feedback from customers and make improvements over time, similar to leveling up your spell.

15. Expansion and Diversification:- Explore opportunities to expand your product line or offer new services, like discovering new spells in the game.

16. Innovation:- Stay creative and look for ways to make your product or service even better, much like discovering hidden features of a spell.

Product or service development is like crafting a powerful tool or magic spell in the online job world. It requires creativity, testing, and continuous improvement to ensure it meets the needs of your customers and helps you succeed in your online job venture.

Building a Strong Online Presence

Think of building a strong online presence as creating a heroic persona in an online game. Here's how it works in online jobs:

1. Choose Your Character: Similar to selecting a character in a game, decide how you want to be seen online. What image do you want to portray?

2. Create Your Avatar: Just as you design your in-game avatar, build your online identity. Create a professional profile or website that reflects who you are.

3. Select Your Platform: Decide where you want to be active online, like choosing the battlegrounds in a game. Pick social media platforms, forums, or websites that suit your goals.

4. Craft Your Story: Develop your story or message, like a character's backstory in a game. Explain what you do, your skills, and how you can help others.

5. Visual Branding: Create a visual brand, like customizing your character's appearance. Use consistent colors, logos, and images to make your online presence recognizable.

6. Content Strategy: Plan what you'll share online, similar to choosing your character's actions in the game. Share valuable content related to your expertise.

7. Engagement Tactics: Interact with your audience, like your character communicating with other players. Respond to comments and messages to build relationships.

8. Consistency: Stay consistent in your online activities, like playing regularly in the game world. Post regularly and stick to your chosen theme.

9. Quality Over Quantity:- Focus on quality, not just quantity, in your online interactions and content, much like aiming for precision in the game.

10. Networking:- Connect with others in your field, similar to joining a guild or a team in a game. Networking can open doors to opportunities.

Building a strong online presence is like crafting a legendary character in an online game. It involves creating a consistent and trustworthy identity that attracts opportunities and helps you excel in your online job endeavors.

Marketing and Promotion Strategies

Think of marketing and promotion strategies as your way of letting the world know about your online job, just like announcing a grand event in a game. Here's how it works in online jobs:

1. Setting Your Goal: Begin by defining your goal, much like setting a quest or mission in a game. What do you want to achieve with your marketing efforts?

2. Understanding Your Audience: Know your target audience, similar to understanding the types of challenges and enemies you'll face in a game level. Who are your potential customers?

3. Creating Valuable Content: Develop content that's useful and interesting to your audience, just as you'd gather helpful items for your character in a game.

4. Choosing the Right Channels: Select the best platforms to reach your audience, like picking the right tools or weapons for your game character.

5. Consistency and Branding: Stay consistent in your messaging and branding, much like having a unique appearance for your game character.

6. Social Media Engagement: Engage with your audience on social media, similar to interacting with other players in a game. Respond to comments and build relationships.

7. Email Marketing: Use email marketing to keep your audience informed, just as you'd send messages to teammates in a game.

8. Search Engine Optimization (SEO): Optimize your online content to be easily found, like discovering hidden treasures in a game.

9. Paid Advertising: Invest in paid advertising if it aligns with your goals, similar to buying useful items or power-ups in a game.

10. Influencer Marketing: Partner with influencers or experts in your field, like joining forces with experienced players in a game.

11. Content Marketing: Share valuable content related to your online job, much like sharing tips and strategies in the gaming community.

12. Public Relations: Build relationships with media and industry influencers, similar to making alliances in a game.

13. Analytics and Data: Use analytics tools to track your marketing performance, just as you'd check your game stats to improve.

14. Customer Testimonials: Share positive feedback and testimonials from satisfied customers, like showcasing your character's achievements in a game.

15. Limited-Time Offers and Promotions: Create special promotions or offers to attract attention, similar to limited-time events or bonuses in a game.

16. Adapt and Learn:
 Adapt your strategies based on what works and what doesn't, like changing tactics when facing different challenges in a game.

Marketing and promotion strategies are like your game plan for conquering the online job world. They help you reach your target audience, attract opportunities, and achieve success in your online job endeavors.

Customer Acquisition Tactics

Think of customer acquisition tactics as the strategies you use to gather teammates or allies in an online game. In online jobs, these tactics help you find and gain new customers. Here's how they work:

1. Defining Your Ideal Customer: Start by knowing who your ideal customer is, like choosing the right teammates with specific abilities in a game.

2. Market Research: Research where your potential customers hang out online, similar to finding locations or hotspots in a game.

3. Content Creation: Create valuable content that speaks to your audience's needs and interests, much like sharing useful items with your teammates in a game.

4. Social Media Presence: Be active on social media platforms where your audience is active, like coordinating with teammates through in-game chat.

5. Search Engine Optimization (SEO): Optimize your online content to be easily found when people search for your services, similar to improving your character's skills.

6. Email Marketing: Use email marketing to keep in touch with potential customers, just like sending messages to fellow players in a game.

7. Networking: Attend online events and webinars to connect with potential customers and industry peers, much like making alliances with other players.

8. Referral Programs: Create referral programs that encourage satisfied customers to bring in new ones, like receiving rewards for recruiting new team members in a game.

9. Paid Advertising: Invest in paid advertising on platforms where your audience spends time, similar to buying powerful equipment or tools in a game.

10. Influencer Partnerships: Partner with influencers or experts in your field to reach their audience, like joining forces with skilled players in a game.

Customer acquisition tactics help you build a team of loyal customers who support your online job journey. By using these strategies, you can expand your reach, connect with potential customers, and ultimately achieve success in your online job endeavors.

Financial Management and Budgeting

Think of financial management and budgeting as the coins and resources you collect and manage in an online game. In online jobs, it's about handling your money wisely. Here's how it works:

1. Income Tracking: Keep track of all the money you earn from your online job, like collecting coins or rewards in a game.

2. Expense Tracking: Monitor where your money goes, similar to keeping an eye on how you spend resources in a game.

3. Budget Creation: Create a budget that outlines your income and planned expenses, just as you'd plan your character's strategy and resources.

4. Emergency Fund: Set aside some money for unexpected expenses, like having backup items or skills for tough game battles.

5. Savings Goals: Define what you're saving for, like achieving specific objectives or acquiring special items in the game.

6. Debt Management: If you have debts, create a plan to manage and reduce them, similar to resolving in-game challenges.

7. Investments: Consider ways to make your money grow, like investing in skills or equipment that enhance your character's abilities.

8. Expense Cutting: Find ways to reduce unnecessary expenses, much like optimizing your gameplay by conserving resources.

9. Regular Reviews: Periodically review your finances, like checking your character's inventory to see what you have.

10. Financial Goals: Set long-term financial goals, such as leveling up your character or completing challenging missions in the game.

Scaling Your Business

Scaling your business in online jobs is like leveling up your character in a game. It's about growing your online job venture to reach more customers and achieve greater success. Here's how it works:

1. Assess Your Current Position: Start by evaluating where your online job stands, much like assessing your character's skills and equipment in a game.

2. Identify Opportunities: Look for opportunities to expand your business, similar to discovering new quests or missions in a game world.

3. Market Research: Conduct market research to understand what your customers want and what your competitors are doing, like gathering intelligence on in-game challenges.

4. Scalability Analysis: Determine if your online job can be scaled without sacrificing quality, much like ensuring your character can handle tougher opponents.

5. Business Plan Revision: Update your business plan to reflect your scaling goals and strategies, similar to planning your character's development in the game.

6. Resource Allocation: Allocate resources, such as time and money, to support your scaling efforts, like distributing resources among your team in a game.

7. Hiring and Team Building: Consider hiring additional help or building a team to handle increased demand, much like recruiting new members for your game party.

8. Automation and Technology: Use technology and automation to streamline processes and increase efficiency, similar to using advanced tools and equipment in the game.

9. Marketing and Promotion: Scale your marketing and promotion efforts to reach a wider audience, like expanding your influence in different game areas.

10. Customer Support: Enhance your customer support to handle a growing customer base, similar to ensuring your team can handle more challenges.

Scaling your business in online jobs is an exciting journey that involves careful planning, resource management, and the pursuit of new opportunities. By leveling up your online job venture, you can reach greater heights and achieve your goals in the online job world.

Adapting to Market Changes

Adapting to market changes in online jobs is like adjusting your strategy in an online game when facing unexpected challenges. It involves staying flexible and responsive to shifts in the online job landscape. Here's how it works:

1. Market Monitoring: Keep a close eye on the online job market, similar to scouting for changes and dangers in a game world.

2. Trends and Insights: Stay informed about industry trends and gather insights into what's happening, much like gathering information about game updates or enemy tactics.

3. Customer Feedback: Listen to feedback from your customers, similar to taking advice from experienced players in the game community.

4. Competitor Analysis: Study your competitors and what they're doing, much like observing the strategies of other players in the game.

5. Flexibility in Strategy: Be ready to adjust your online job strategy when needed, just as you'd change your tactics in the game to adapt to different situations.

6. Diversification: Consider diversifying your services or products to meet changing demands, like acquiring new skills or abilities in the game.

7. Technology Adoption: Embrace new technologies and tools that can enhance your online job, similar to acquiring new weapons or tools in the game.

8. Customer-Centric Approach: Focus on meeting the evolving needs of your customers, much like tailoring your gameplay to succeed in different game scenarios.

9. Agility and Speed: Be agile and act swiftly when market changes occur, just as you'd react quickly to in-game challenges.

10. Cost Management: Manage your costs efficiently to maintain profitability, similar to managing your in-game resources to avoid running out.

Adapting to market changes in online jobs is essential for long-term success. By staying vigilant, flexible, and responsive, you can navigate the evolving online job landscape and continue to thrive in your online job journey.

Networking and Industry Connections

Networking and industry connections in online jobs are like building alliances and relationships with other players in an online game. They help you connect with professionals, learn from others, and open doors to opportunities. Here's how it works:

1. Building Relationships: Start by building genuine relationships with people in your industry, similar to making friends and allies in a game world.

2. Online Platforms: Use online platforms like social media, forums, and industry-specific websites to connect with others, much like interacting with players on game servers.

3. LinkedIn: Create a professional LinkedIn profile to showcase your skills and connect with professionals, similar to displaying your character's abilities and achievements.

4. Networking Events: Attend online networking events and webinars, just as you'd join in-game gatherings or events.

5. Industry Associations: Join industry associations or groups to connect with like-minded professionals, like joining a guild or club in the game.

6. Sharing Knowledge: Share your knowledge and expertise with others in your field, much like helping other players by sharing tips and strategies in the game community.

7. Learning from Peers: Learn from your industry peers and stay updated on industry trends, similar to learning new tactics and strategies from fellow players in the game.

8. Collaboration Opportunities: Explore collaboration opportunities with others in your network, like teaming up with other players for in-game missions.

9. Mentorship: Seek mentorship from experienced professionals, similar to learning from seasoned players in the game.

10. Job Referrals: Networking can lead to job referrals and recommendations, much like getting recruited for specific roles in the game.

Networking and industry connections are valuable assets in your online job journey. They provide you with a supportive community, access to knowledge, and opportunities for growth, much like forming alliances and friendships enhance your experience in an online game.

CHAPTER 6

THRIVING AS A VIRTUAL ASSISTANT AND REMOTE SUPPORT PRO

Thriving as a virtual assistant and remote support professional in online jobs is like excelling in a specific role within an online game. It involves providing valuable assistance and support to businesses or individuals remotely. Thriving in the role of a virtual assistant and remote support professional involves efficiently managing tasks, providing excellent service, and continuously improving your skills to meet the demands of the online job world.

Virtual Assistant Roles and Responsibilities

Imagine being the go-to helper in a big online game. That's a bit like being a virtual assistant in the world of online jobs. Here's what virtual assistants do and what they're responsible for:

1. Administrative Tasks: Virtual assistants handle administrative stuff, like organizing schedules, managing emails, and setting up appointments. It's like being the organizer in a game, keeping everything in order.

2. Data Entry: They might also deal with data entry, which is like inputting important information into a game system, keeping track of scores or items.

3. Customer Support: Providing customer support is another job. It's like helping fellow players in the game when they have questions or need assistance.

4. Social Media Management: Some virtual assistants manage social media accounts for businesses, similar to having in-game characters with specific roles and skills.

5. Content Creation: They might create content like blog posts or graphics, much like creating content or resources for fellow players in a game.

6. Research: Research is also part of the job. They gather information, a bit like scouting for new areas or quests in a game.

7. Email Correspondence: They communicate with clients or customers through email, similar to sending messages or chatting with other players in the game.

8. Project Management: Some virtual assistants manage projects, making sure things are progressing smoothly, like leading a group in a game mission.

9. Bookkeeping: Handling finances, like keeping track of game currency or resources, is another responsibility.

10. Travel Planning: They might even plan travel arrangements for clients, much like arranging journeys or adventures in a game.

11. Meeting Coordination: Coordinating meetings and making sure everyone's on the same page is part of the role, similar to organizing team meetings in a game.

12. Tech Assistance: They provide technical support, helping clients with software or tools, like having the skills to troubleshoot in-game issues.

So, being a virtual assistant in online jobs is a bit like being a helpful and versatile player in an online game, taking on various roles and responsibilities to support others in their online endeavors.

Setting Up Your Remote Office

Setting up your remote office for online jobs is like creating your own special gaming space. It's where you'll work, be productive, and feel comfortable. Here's how to do it:

1. Choose Your Workspace: Pick a quiet and comfortable spot at home, just like finding a cozy corner in your gaming room.

2. Furniture and Equipment: Get the right furniture and equipment, like a desk, chair, and computer. It's like having a gaming chair and a powerful gaming computer for the best experience.

3. Internet Connection: Make sure you have a stable internet connection, just like a gamer needs a strong connection to play smoothly.

4. Lighting: Good lighting is important, so you can work comfortably, like ensuring your gaming area is well-lit for gaming sessions.

5. Organize Cables: Keep cables tidy to avoid clutter, similar to organizing your gaming setup to keep things neat.

6. Ergonomics: Set up your workspace ergonomically, so you're comfortable and avoid strain, just like adjusting your gaming setup for comfort during long play sessions.

7. Storage: Have storage for your work materials and tools, similar to storing your gaming accessories and gear.

8. Noise Management: If it's noisy, use headphones or noise-cancelling tools, like blocking out external noise for a peaceful gaming experience.

9. Personal Touch: Add personal touches like plants or decorations to make your workspace enjoyable, much like adding posters or collectibles to your gaming area.

10. Daily Routine: Create a daily work routine, so you have a schedule, like setting specific gaming times.

11. Distraction-Free Zone: Make it a distraction-free zone during work hours, just as you'd have focused gaming sessions.

12. Communication Tools: Set up communication tools like video conferencing, similar to using in-game chat or voice chat with teammates.

13. Backup Plan: Have a backup plan for power outages or technical issues, like having a backup battery for your gaming devices.

14. Security: Ensure cybersecurity to protect your work, similar to securing your gaming account from hacking.

15. Personal Comfort: Finally, make your remote office a place where you feel comfortable and motivated to work, like your gaming setup where you enjoy playing.

Setting up your remote office is all about creating a productive and comfortable space for your online job journey, much like setting up your gaming area for immersive gaming experiences.

Effective Time Management Techniques

Managing your time wisely in online jobs is like solving puzzles in a video game. Here's a straightforward guide to help you make the most of your time:

1. Prioritize Your Tasks: Just as you prioritize completing critical tasks in a game, identify your most important work and tackle it first.

2. Set Clear Goals: Define clear goals for your work, similar to having clear objectives in a game. Knowing what you want to accomplish helps you stay focused.

3. Use a Calendar: Employ a digital calendar or planner to schedule your work tasks and deadlines, like keeping track of your gaming missions.

4. Time Blocking: Allocate specific time blocks for different tasks or projects, much like allocating time for different in-game activities.

5. Avoid Multitasking: Avoid juggling multiple tasks at once, as it can lead to errors. Focus on one task at a time, just as you focus on one game challenge at a time.

6. Take Regular Breaks: Take short breaks to recharge, similar to taking breaks during a gaming session. Short rests can boost productivity.

7. Minimize Distractions: Reduce distractions like social media or unrelated games, much like turning off unrelated apps or notifications while gaming.

8. Track Your Time: Use time-tracking tools to monitor how you spend your working hours, similar to checking your in-game stats to assess your progress.

9. Set Realistic Deadlines: Establish achievable deadlines for your tasks, much like setting deadlines for completing game objectives.

10. Learn to Say No: Don't overcommit to tasks or projects. Decline additional work if your plate is already full, similar to declining extra quests in a game.

Effective time management in online jobs is all about staying organized, setting clear objectives, and optimizing your working hours, just like strategizing and solving puzzles in a video game to progress.

Communication Skills for Remote Work

Think of communication skills in remote work for online jobs like mastering the language of a video game. Here's a straightforward guide to help you improve your communication:

1. Clear and Concise Messages: Just as you need to communicate your intentions clearly in a game, ensure your messages are straightforward and concise. Avoid unnecessary jargon or lengthy explanations.

2. Active Listening: Actively listen to what others are saying, similar to paying attention to game instructions or dialogues. Show you're engaged by asking questions and providing feedback.

3. Use Appropriate Tone: Choose the right tone for your messages. Be friendly and professional, like maintaining a respectful tone in a multiplayer game.

4. Email Etiquette: Follow email etiquette by using subject lines, addressing recipients properly, and proofreading your messages, just as you'd follow game rules and guidelines.

5. Video and Audio Calls: When on video or audio calls, ensure you have a quiet background and clear audio, like having a stable in-game environment for better communication.

6. Effective Written Communication: Write well-structured emails and messages. Use bullet points or numbered lists for clarity, similar to using effective strategies in the game.

7. Timely Responses: Respond to messages and emails promptly, much like quickly reacting to in-game events to stay competitive.

8. Collaboration Tools: Familiarize yourself with collaboration tools like Slack or Microsoft

Teams, similar to using in-game communication tools to coordinate with teammates.

9. Feedback and Constructive Criticism: Provide feedback and constructive criticism respectfully, just as you'd offer tips or guidance to fellow players in a game.

10. Conflict Resolution: Address conflicts professionally and work toward solutions, similar to resolving disputes among players in the game.

Effective communication skills are vital in online jobs, helping you work efficiently and collaborate with remote teams, much like mastering in-game communication to excel and progress in the gaming world.

Building a Professional Online Presence

Creating a professional online presence for online jobs is similar to crafting your character's image in a video game. Here's a straightforward guide to help you build and maintain your online presence:

1. Professional Profile: Just as you create a character with a unique look, set up a professional online profile. Use a clear photo and a concise bio.

2. LinkedIn and Online Portfolios: Consider creating a LinkedIn profile and an online portfolio. It's like showcasing your character's skills and achievements in a game.

3. Consistent Branding: Maintain consistent branding across platforms, similar to how you maintain a consistent character identity in the gaming community.

4. Content Sharing: Share relevant content related to your field, like sharing game-related content in gaming communities.

5. Engagement: Engage with your network by commenting on posts and participating in discussions, similar to engaging with fellow players in the game.

6. Professional Email Address: Use a professional email address for work-related communication, like choosing a character name that suits the game world.

7. Online Courses and Certifications: Enroll in online courses or certifications to enhance your skills, similar to leveling up your character by acquiring new abilities in the game.

8. Networking: Network with professionals in your field, just as you form alliances or join guilds in the gaming world.

9. Regular Updates: Keep your profile and information up to date, similar to maintaining your character's gear and stats in the game.

10. Online Etiquette: Follow online etiquette by being respectful and professional in your interactions, like adhering to gaming community rules.

Building a professional online presence is essential in online jobs, as it helps you connect with potential clients and employers, much like creating a strong character presence in the gaming world to interact and succeed in the game.

Client Relationship Management

Client relationship management in online jobs is like building trust and camaraderie with teammates in a multiplayer video game. Here's a straightforward guide to help you manage your client relationships effectively:

1. Clear Communication: Just as clear communication is crucial in teamwork, ensure you communicate with clients effectively. Understand their needs and expectations.

2. Setting Expectations: Set clear expectations from the start, similar to outlining game objectives before starting a mission.

3. Regular Updates: Provide regular updates on your progress, much like reporting in-game progress to your team.

4. Meeting Deadlines: Always meet deadlines, just as punctuality is important in multiplayer gaming.

5. Quality Work: Deliver high-quality work, similar to contributing effectively to your team's success in a game.

6. Feedback Loop: Create a feedback loop where you and the client can discuss improvements and changes, like strategizing with your gaming team.

7. Conflict Resolution: Address conflicts professionally and find resolutions, similar to resolving disputes among teammates in the game.

8. Building Trust: Build trust over time by consistently delivering excellent results, much like earning your teammates' trust through skilled gameplay.

9. Professionalism: Maintain professionalism in all interactions, like maintaining sportsmanship in multiplayer gaming.

10. Transparency: Be transparent about any issues or delays, similar to informing your team about obstacles in a game.

Client relationship management in online jobs is about building strong, mutually beneficial partnerships, much like fostering teamwork and camaraderie in multiplayer gaming for shared success.

Problem-Solving in Remote Work

Problem-solving in remote work for online jobs is similar to tackling challenges and puzzles in a video game. Here's a straightforward guide to help you become an effective problem solver:

1. Identifying the Problem: Just as you recognize obstacles or challenges in a game, start by identifying the problem you need to solve in your work.

2. Gather Information: Gather all relevant information about the problem, similar to collecting clues and hints in a game.

3. Analyze the Situation: Analyze the situation and break down the problem into smaller parts, much like dissecting complex game levels.

4. Brainstorm Solutions:

Brainstorm potential solutions to the problem, just as you brainstorm strategies to overcome obstacles in a game.

5. Evaluate Options: Evaluate each solution's pros and cons, similar to considering different tactics in the game.

6. Choose the Best Solution: Select the most suitable solution, like picking the best strategy to progress in the game.

7. Implement the Solution: Put your chosen solution into action, much like executing your chosen game plan.

8. Monitor Progress: Keep an eye on how your solution is working, similar to assessing your progress in the game.

9. Adjust as Needed: If the solution isn't working as expected, be ready to make adjustments, like adapting your gameplay when facing unexpected challenges.

10. Seek Help When Necessary: Don't hesitate to seek assistance or guidance from colleagues or supervisors, similar to asking fellow gamers for advice.

Problem-solving in remote work involves critical thinking and adaptability, much like mastering in-game challenges and puzzles to progress.

Balancing Multiple Clients and Tasks

Balancing multiple clients and tasks in online jobs is akin to managing various missions and quests in a video game. Here's a straightforward guide to help you excel at juggling different responsibilities:

1. Prioritization: Just as you prioritize quests and objectives in a game, prioritize your clients and tasks based on deadlines and importance.

2. Task Organization: Organize your tasks efficiently, similar to arranging your inventory or managing quests in a game.

3. Time Management: Manage your time effectively by allocating specific time slots for each client or task, much like planning your gameplay sessions.

4. Use Tools and Apps: Utilize productivity tools and apps to track tasks and deadlines, similar to using in-game tools for navigation or resource management.

5. Set Realistic Goals: Set achievable goals for each task or client, just as you set achievable goals in a game to avoid overwhelm.

6. Avoid Multitasking: Refrain from multitasking excessively. Focus on one task at a time, similar to concentrating on one game challenge to succeed.

7. Clear Communication: Keep communication clear with clients about your workload and deadlines, like communicating with fellow gamers about your role in team missions.

8. Delegate When Possible: If feasible, delegate tasks or seek assistance, similar to teaming up with other players to tackle difficult game levels.

9. Time Blocks for Breaks: Allocate short breaks between tasks to recharge, similar to taking short breaks during gaming sessions to stay alert.

10. Flexibility: Stay flexible and adapt to changing priorities, just as you adapt to dynamic game scenarios.

Balancing multiple clients and tasks in online jobs requires effective organization and time management, similar to orchestrating various aspects of gameplay in a video game to achieve success.

Staying Organized and Productive

Staying organized and productive in online jobs is like keeping your game character efficient and well-prepared for every mission. Here's a simple guide to help you excel in this area:

1. Task List: Just as you have a quest log in games, maintain a task list with all your work assignments and deadlines.

2. Prioritization: Prioritize tasks based on their importance and deadlines, similar to prioritizing quests in a game.

3. Daily Schedule: Create a daily schedule that outlines when you'll work on specific tasks, much like planning your gaming sessions.

4. Dedicated Workspace: Set up a dedicated workspace, like your character's base camp in a game, where you can focus without distractions.

5. Use Productivity Tools: Utilize productivity tools and apps to help you manage tasks, just as you use in-game tools to navigate or track resources.

6. Breaks and Rest: Include short breaks in your schedule to rest and recharge, similar to resting your character in the game to regain strength.

7. Avoid Multitasking: Avoid multitasking excessively. Focus on one task at a time, much like tackling one game challenge at a time for success.

8. Regular Updates: Keep clients or supervisors updated on your progress, similar to giving team updates during multiplayer gaming.

9. Time Blocks for Emails: Allocate specific time blocks for checking and responding to emails, like handling in-game messages during specific intervals.

10. Minimize Distractions: Minimize distractions by silencing notifications and creating a focused work environment, similar to finding a quiet spot for gaming.

Staying organized and productive in online jobs involves effective planning and self-discipline, much like optimizing your game character's abilities and resources for a victorious gaming experience.

Professional Development and Training

Professional development and training in online jobs are like leveling up your skills and abilities in a video game. Here's a simple guide to help you understand and excel in this aspect:

1. Skill Enhancement: Just as you improve your character's skills in a game, focus on enhancing your professional skills. Identify areas where you can grow.

2. Continuous Learning: Engage in continuous learning, similar to acquiring new abilities or knowledge in the game world. Stay updated with industry trends.

3. Online Courses: Explore online courses and resources that can help you develop your skills, like finding power-ups or items to boost your character in a game.

4. Certifications: Consider obtaining certifications in your field, much like achieving badges or titles in a game to demonstrate your expertise.

5. Networking: Build a professional network by connecting with colleagues and industry experts, similar to forming alliances with other players in the gaming community.

6. Mentorship: Seek mentorship or guidance from experienced professionals, just as you might receive guidance from experienced gamers.

7. Practice and Application: Apply what you learn in real work scenarios, similar to using new skills and strategies in actual game missions.

8. Feedback and Improvement: Welcome feedback and use it to improve, much like analyzing your gameplay and making adjustments for better performance.

9. Webinars and Workshops: Attend webinars and workshops to gain insights and interact with experts, like participating in in-game events for rewards and knowledge.

10. Industry Conferences: Participate in industry conferences or conventions to stay informed and connect with professionals, similar to attending gaming conventions for updates and socializing.

Professional development and training in online jobs involve continuous growth and improvement, much like evolving your character's skills and abilities for success in the game.

Time Management Tools and Software

Time management tools and software in online jobs are like magical items that help you organize and use your time wisely in a video game. Here's a simple guide to understanding and making the most of these tools:

1. Overview of Tools: Just as you gather items in a game, learn about time management tools and software available to you. These can include calendars, task lists, and productivity apps.

2. Calendar Apps: Calendar apps are like quest logs. They help you schedule work tasks and personal activities. Use them to plan your day, set reminders, and track important dates.

3. Task Lists: Task lists are your to-do lists in the game. They help you break down your work into manageable tasks. Use digital task list apps to organize and prioritize your workload.

4. Project Management Tools: Project management tools are like treasure maps. They guide you through complex projects, much like navigating through challenging game levels. These tools help you assign tasks, set deadlines, and track progress.

5. Time Tracking Software: Time tracking software is your stopwatch in the game. It records how much time you spend on different tasks, helping you evaluate your productivity and manage your time better.

6. Collaboration Platforms: Collaboration platforms are your team's communication hub, much like a party chat in a game. They enable real-time communication, file sharing, and collaborative work with teammates.

7. Automation Tools: Automation tools are like magical spells that can perform repetitive tasks for you. Use them to automate email responses, data entry, or social media posts, freeing up your time for more important tasks.

8. Cloud Storage Solutions: Cloud storage is your inventory bag. It lets you store and access your work documents and files from anywhere, similar to having all your game items accessible at any location.

9. Note-Taking Apps: Note-taking apps are your journal in the game. Use them to jot down ideas, meeting notes, and important information. They help you stay organized and never forget important details.

10. Productivity Apps: Productivity apps are like power-ups. They can block distracting websites, track your screen time, and even provide insights into your work habits, helping you stay focused.

Time management tools and software are your allies in the online job world, helping you become more organized, efficient, and productive, much like using special items and abilities to conquer challenges in a video game.

CHAPTER 7

UNLOCKING THE WORLD OF INNOVATIVE ONLINE CAREERS

The world of work is in the midst of a profound transformation. Traditional career paths are no longer the only option, and the rise of the digital age has ushered in a new era of innovative online careers. The internet, once a tool for communication and information, has evolved into a platform that offers a diverse and dynamic array of career opportunities. In this essay, we will embark on a journey to explore the exciting landscape of innovative online careers. We will delve into the factors driving this transformation, the various paths available, and the skills and mindset required to succeed in this ever-evolving digital realm.

The Digital Revolution: Catalyst for Change

The digital revolution, characterized by the widespread adoption of the internet, mobile devices, and digital technologies, has been the driving force behind the emergence of innovative online careers. This revolution has fundamentally altered the way we live, communicate, and conduct business. It has connected people across the globe, breaking down geographical barriers and creating a global marketplace for talent.

The increased connectivity and accessibility to digital tools have empowered individuals to explore new career paths. The internet has become a virtual playground where creative minds can thrive. As a result, traditional constraints, such as location and access to resources, have been largely overcome. In this new era, innovative online careers have become a viable and attractive option for those seeking opportunities beyond the confines of traditional employment.

The Diversity of Online Careers

One of the defining features of innovative online careers is their diversity. There is no one-size-fits-all approach in this digital landscape. Instead, individuals have the freedom to choose from a wide range of career options that align with their passions, skills, and aspirations. Let's explore some of the most prominent online career paths:

Freelancing: Freelancers, often referred to as "digital nomads," have embraced the freedom and flexibility of working on their terms. They offer a wide range of services, from writing and graphic design to programming and digital marketing. Freelancers can tap into a global clientele and build their portfolios, all from the comfort of their chosen location.

Digital Entrepreneurship: Entrepreneurs have leveraged the power of the internet to create and grow their online businesses. E-commerce stores, digital marketing agencies, and software startups are just a few examples of the diverse ventures that have emerged in the digital realm. The barriers to entry are lower than ever, making it possible for individuals to turn their ideas into profitable online enterprises.

Remote Work: The traditional office is no longer a necessity. Remote work has become a defining feature of the modern workforce, allowing individuals to work from anywhere in the world. This shift has not only increased flexibility but has also opened up opportunities for collaboration on a global scale. Professionals can now contribute to projects and teams regardless of geographical constraints.

Gig Economy: The gig economy has redefined the nature of work, offering short-term, project-based opportunities that cater to a variety of skills and talents. Gig workers can take on a range of tasks, from delivering groceries to providing freelance services. This dynamic and fast-paced sector of the job market provides flexibility and autonomy.

Skills and Mindset for Success

To unlock the full potential of innovative online careers, individuals must possess a unique set of skills and a forward-thinking mindset. These careers are often characterized by their merit-based approach, where success is determined by one's ability to acquire and apply relevant skills. Let's explore the essential skills and mindset required for success:

Continuous Learning: The digital landscape evolves rapidly, demanding continuous learning and adaptation. Online professionals must stay up-to-date with industry trends and emerging technologies. Embracing a lifelong learning mindset is crucial for remaining relevant and competitive.

Digital Literacy: Proficiency in digital tools and technologies is essential. Online professionals must be comfortable navigating digital platforms, using productivity software, and leveraging online resources for skill development.

Adaptability: Change is constant in the digital world. Online professionals must embrace change and view challenges as opportunities for growth. Adaptability is a prized trait, allowing individuals to pivot and adjust their strategies in response to shifting market dynamics.

Self-Discipline: The freedom and autonomy offered by online careers require self-discipline. Professionals must be able to manage their time effectively, set priorities, and stay focused on their goals. Developing strong self-discipline is essential for maintaining productivity and achieving long-term success.

Effective Communication: Online careers often involve remote collaboration and communication. Effective communication skills, both written and verbal, are critical for building relationships with clients, colleagues, and partners. Clear and concise communication fosters trust and ensures successful project outcomes.

Entrepreneurial Mindset: Many online professionals embrace an entrepreneurial mindset, even if they don't own their businesses. This mindset involves a willingness to take calculated risks, innovate, and seize opportunities. It also involves resilience in the face of setbacks and failures.

Problem-Solving Skills: In the digital realm, problem-solving skills are invaluable. Professionals must be adept at identifying challenges, analyzing situations, and developing creative solutions. Problem-solving abilities enable individuals to navigate complex digital landscapes effectively.

Networking and Collaboration: Building a professional network and collaborating with others are essential components of online careers. Networking allows professionals to connect with like-minded individuals, seek mentorship, and discover new opportunities. Collaboration enhances creativity and results in innovative solutions.

Innovative online careers have emerged as a vibrant and exciting aspect of the contemporary job market. The digital revolution, marked by increased connectivity and accessibility to digital tools, has paved the way for a diverse range of career opportunities. From freelancing to digital entrepreneurship, remote work to the gig economy, these careers offer flexibility, autonomy, and a chance to pursue one's passions.

Success in the world of innovative online careers requires a unique set of skills and a forward-thinking mindset. Continuous learning, digital literacy, adaptability, self-discipline, effective communication, and an entrepreneurial spirit are among the essential attributes for thriving in this digital landscape. Moreover, the ability to solve problems, build professional networks, and collaborate with others is crucial for unlocking the full potential of online careers.

As we navigate this transformative era, individuals have the opportunity to redefine their careers and unlock their full potential in the world of innovative online careers. The digital revolution has opened doors to a world of possibilities, and those who embrace this new era of work are poised for success in an ever-evolving digital realm.

CHAPTER 8

THE ART OF ONLINE TEACHING AND TUTORING

The world of education has changed a lot in recent times. One of the big changes is online teaching and tutoring. This means that teachers and tutors can now teach and help students using the internet. It's a bit like going to school, but instead of sitting in a classroom, you sit in front of a computer or a tablet. In this essay, we will look closely at online teaching and tutoring. We'll talk about why it's important, what makes a good online teacher or tutor, and how technology helps in online education. We'll also talk about the challenges and how we can solve them. Finally, we'll see how online tutoring can make a big difference for students.

Why Online Teaching and Tutoring?

Let's start by understanding why online teaching and tutoring are becoming so important. One big reason is that it allows students to learn from anywhere. Imagine you live in a small town with no good schools. With online education, you can still get a good education. It doesn't matter if you're in a big city or a small village. Another reason is that it's flexible. This means you can choose when you want to learn. If you're a night owl, you can study at night. If you prefer mornings, you can do your lessons then. Online teaching and tutoring also open doors to many different subjects. You can learn almost anything online, from math and science to art and music. It's like having a whole world of knowledge at your fingertips.

What Makes a Great Online Teacher or Tutor?

Being a good online teacher or tutor is a bit different from being a teacher in a classroom.

You need some special skills. First, you need to make your lessons interesting. Imagine watching a movie with no action or fun – it would be boring! The same goes for lessons. A great online teacher knows how to make learning fun and exciting. Second, you need to be patient. Some students might need more time to understand things, and that's okay. A good online teacher doesn't rush and is always ready to help. Third, you have to be clear in your explanations. Remember, you can't see your students face-to-face, so you need to explain things very well. Fourth, being friendly and approachable is essential. Students should feel comfortable asking questions and seeking help when needed. Finally, a good online teacher or tutor is tech-savvy. You should know how to use computers and the internet well because they are your tools for teaching.

Technology and Online Education

Technology plays a big role in online teaching and tutoring. It's like the magic wand that makes everything possible. Computers, tablets, and the internet connect teachers and students. Learning management systems (LMS) are like virtual classrooms where lessons and assignments are organized. Video conferencing tools allow students and teachers to see and hear each other in real-time. These tools make online education feel like a real classroom, even if students and teachers are far apart. Moreover, technology can adapt to each student's needs. For example, some programs can give students extra practice in areas they struggle with. Technology is like a friendly assistant, helping teachers and students in their online journey.

Challenges and Solutions

Online teaching and tutoring have some challenges too. One big challenge is keeping students engaged and motivated. Without a physical classroom, students may feel lonely or lose interest. To solve this, teachers can use interactive lessons, discussions, and group activities to keep students engaged. Another challenge is distractions. At home, students might have TVs, games, and family members around. Teachers and parents can help by creating a quiet and distraction-free study space. Sometimes, students may also have technical issues, like poor internet connections. Teachers can provide recordings of lessons so students can watch them later if they miss something. Clear communication between teachers, students, and parents is vital to overcome these challenges.

The Impact of Online Tutoring

Online tutoring is like having a personal coach for learning. It can make a big difference for students. Whether you need help with math, language, or preparing for exams, there's an online tutor for you. Online tutoring can be one-on-one or in small groups, so you get special attention. It's like having a teacher just for you. This helps students understand better and do well in their studies. Online tutoring is also flexible. You can schedule sessions when it suits you. For busy students, this is a big advantage.

Moreover, online tutoring is not limited by borders. You can have a tutor from another country who speaks a different language, and it's still possible to learn from them. It opens doors to a world of knowledge and expertise.

In conclusion, the art of online teaching and tutoring is changing the way we learn and teach. It makes education accessible to everyone, no matter where they are. Good online teachers and tutors have special skills, like making lessons interesting and being patient. Technology is the backbone of online education, connecting teachers and students. However, there are challenges like keeping students engaged and dealing with distractions. Online tutoring is a powerful tool that can help students excel in their studies. It's flexible, personalized, and opens up a world of opportunities. With the right tools and approaches, online teaching and tutoring have the potential to revolutionize education and make learning a truly enjoyable and enriching experience for all.

CHAPTER 9

EXPLORING EXCITING NEW HORIZONS IN ONLINE EMPLOYMENT

The landscape of employment has undergone a remarkable transformation with the advent of the internet and the proliferation of online jobs. This essay embarks on a journey to delve into the multifaceted realm of online employment, charting the course of its growth, its diverse array of opportunities, the skills that light the way to success, and the myriad challenges and advantages that await those who venture into this dynamic field.

The Dawn of Online Employment

The rise of online employment represents a paradigm shift in the way we work and earn a living. This transformation has been fueled by several factors. First and foremost, the internet has woven a tapestry of connectivity that spans the globe, enabling individuals to collaborate with employers, clients, and colleagues from all corners of the world. Geographical boundaries have blurred, opening doors to a global job market. Second, the digital age has ushered in an era of heightened demand for online services, giving birth to a kaleidoscope of job opportunities. From e-commerce and digital marketing to content creation and remote support, the internet has engendered an explosion of job categories. Finally, the COVID-19 pandemic, which disrupted traditional workplaces, accelerated the migration towards remote work. Online employment became not just an option but a necessity for businesses across various industries. As a result, online employment has ascended as a promising avenue for those seeking novel horizons in their careers.

The Vast Canvas of Online Job Diversity

Online employment presents a vast and diverse panorama of job categories, offering a niche for every skill set and passion. The canvas of online work is painted with a myriad of roles, each catering to distinct talents and interests. Among the common online jobs, freelancing stands tall, encompassing a multitude of professions such as graphic design, software development, and digital marketing. Freelancers serve a global clientele, crafting a bridge between talent and demand. Virtual assistants, on the other hand, navigate the realm of administrative support, offering services that transcend borders. The realm of online education has witnessed a meteoric rise, with educators providing lessons to students around the world. Content writers breathe life into blogs, articles, and web content, while e-commerce experts orchestrate online stores and product marketing. These are just a few strokes on the canvas of online employment, with countless other opportunities awaiting discovery.

The Palette of Skills for Success

Success in the world of online employment demands a unique set of skills and qualities, akin to the vibrant colors on an artist's palette. Firstly, digital literacy is a fundamental skill, as online workers navigate a digital landscape replete with software, platforms, and tools. Proficiency in effective written communication is paramount, as the majority of interactions occur through emails, instant messages, or video calls. Time management and self-discipline are essential attributes, given that online workers often define their work schedules. Adaptability is another brushstroke, allowing individuals to remain agile in the face of evolving technology and industry trends. Furthermore, online employment often requires specialized skills tailored to specific job categories, such as coding for programmers or design prowess for graphic artists. The combination of these skills and qualities paints the canvas of success in the online employment realm.

Navigating the Seas of Challenges and Benefits

While online employment promises a voyage of opportunities, it is not without its share of challenges. The digital workspace can be isolating, with the absence of physical colleagues and face-to-face interactions. Loneliness and disconnection can erode morale if not addressed. Additionally, the home environment may harbor distractions, potentially hampering productivity. Cybersecurity concerns loom on the horizon, as online workers handle sensitive data that may be vulnerable to breaches. However, the benefits of online employment often tip the scales in favor of this dynamic field. Flexibility in work hours and location empowers individuals to sculpt a work-life balance that aligns with their preferences. The elimination of daily commutes and office politics translates to enhanced job satisfaction. The potential for a global clientele translates into increased earning potential. Moreover, the rich diversity of online job categories allows individuals to tailor their work to their personal passions. Ultimately, the canvas of online employment presents a compelling tapestry of challenges and benefits, inviting those with the vision to navigate its seas.

A Future of Endless Horizons

In conclusion, the realm of online employment beckons with exciting new horizons, offering a transformative avenue for individuals to shape their careers in the digital age. The internet's global reach, the burgeoning demand for online services, and the accelerated shift towards remote work have coalesced to elevate online employment as a vibrant and dynamic facet of the modern job market. This transformation casts a wide net, accommodating a diverse range of skills and aspirations, from freelancing and virtual assistance to online teaching and e-commerce. Success in this sphere is marked by a palette of skills, including digital literacy, effective communication, time management, adaptability, and specialized expertise. While challenges such as isolation and distractions persist, the allure of flexibility, increased earning potential, and job satisfaction draws aspiring online workers into its fold. As the digital landscape continues to evolve, the world of online employment promises endless horizons, inviting intrepid explorers to embark on a journey of discovery, innovation, and fulfillment.

CHAPTER 10
TRIUMPHS IN THE DIGITAL ARENA

Real-Life Stories of Success in Online Work

The digital arena has emerged as a bustling marketplace of opportunity, where individuals harness the power of the internet to forge successful careers. This essay embarks on a journey through the inspiring tales of individuals who have triumphed in the world of online work. These real-life stories serve as beacons of hope, illuminating the pathways to success in the digital age. We explore the diverse narratives of online entrepreneurs, remote workers, freelancers, and educators, showcasing the limitless possibilities and the common threads of dedication, innovation, and resilience that unite these triumphs.

The Rise of Online Entrepreneurs

The digital realm has witnessed a surge in entrepreneurial spirit, with individuals seizing the opportunity to create and grow online businesses. Take, for example, Sarah, a passionate baker who transformed her love for creating delectable treats into a thriving e-commerce venture. Through a well-designed website and engaging social media presence, she attracted a global customer base. Sarah's story illustrates how online entrepreneurship allows individuals to turn their hobbies and passions into profitable enterprises. Her success story underscores the importance of embracing technology, marketing prowess, and customer engagement.

Remote Work Success Stories

The remote work landscape has become a haven for professionals seeking flexibility and balance in their careers. David, a seasoned software developer, discovered the benefits of remote work when he joined a tech company that embraced a distributed workforce model. This shift allowed him to work from his preferred location while collaborating with an international team. David's journey exemplifies the advantages of remote work, including increased productivity, reduced commuting stress, and the ability to work on projects that align with personal interests. His success story serves as a testament to the growing appeal of remote employment in the digital age.

Thriving in the Freelance World

Freelancers have found their niche in the online job market, offering a wide range of services to clients worldwide. Lisa, a freelance graphic designer, embarked on her freelancing journey after years of working in traditional office settings. Her story showcases the freedom and flexibility that freelancing offers. Lisa can now choose projects that align with her skills and interests, set her own work hours, and enjoy a work-life balance that was elusive in her previous job. Her triumph in the freelance world underscores the potential for individuals to craft their own paths to success through online work.

Educators in the Digital Classroom

Online teaching and tutoring have become transformative avenues for educators. Emma, a dedicated teacher with a passion for mathematics, embraced online teaching platforms to reach students worldwide. Her story highlights how online education transcends geographical boundaries, allowing educators to make a global impact. Emma's students hail from diverse backgrounds, each benefiting from personalized learning experiences. Her journey exemplifies the adaptability of educators in the digital classroom and the potential for innovation in online pedagogy.

Common Threads of Triumph

While these stories represent different facets of online work, common threads of dedication, innovation, and resilience weave through each narrative. Successful individuals in the digital arena share a commitment to honing their skills, embracing technology, and continuously learning and adapting. They exhibit resilience in the face of challenges and demonstrate the creativity to leverage online platforms for growth. These commonalities serve as valuable lessons for aspiring online workers, illustrating that triumph in the digital age is within reach for those who dare to dream and work diligently towards their goals.

In conclusion, the digital arena has witnessed remarkable triumphs as individuals across diverse fields have found success in online work. These real-life stories showcase the boundless opportunities that the internet offers, from online entrepreneurship and remote work to freelancing and online education. The narratives of Sarah, David, Lisa, and Emma serve as beacons of hope, illuminating the pathways to success in the digital age. While their journeys differ, the common threads of dedication, innovation, and resilience unite these triumphs. Aspiring online workers can draw inspiration from these stories, knowing that success in the digital arena is attainable through passion, perseverance, and the embrace of technology. The digital age is a realm of endless possibilities, where the triumphs of today are but the stepping stones to the victories of tomorrow.